T0212658

Lecture Notes in Computer Science 8391

Commenced Publication in 1973
Founding and Former Series Editors:
Gerhard Goos, Juris Hartmanis, and Jan van Leeuwen

Raghunath Nambiar   Meikel Poess (Eds.)

Performance Characterization and Benchmarking

5th TPC Technology Conference, TPCTC 2013
Trento, Italy, August 26, 2013
Revised Selected Papers

 Springer

Volume Editors

Raghunath Nambiar
Cisco Systems, Inc.
Data Center Business Group
275 East Tasman Drive, San Jose, CA 95134, USA
E-mail: rnambiar@cisco.com

Meikel Poess
Oracle Corporation
Server Technologies
500 Oracle Parkway, Redwood Shores, CA 94065, USA
E-mail: meikel.poess@oracle.com

ISSN 0302-9743   e-ISSN 1611-3349
ISBN 978-3-319-04935-9   ISBN 978-3-319-04936-6 (eBook)
DOI 10.1007/978-3-319-04936-6
Springer Cham Heidelberg New York Dordrecht London

Library of Congress Control Number: 2014930885

LNCS Sublibrary: SL 2 – Programming and Software Engineering

Typesetting: Camera-ready by author, data conversion by Scientific Publishing Services, Chennai, India

Printed on acid-free paper

Springer is part of Springer Science+Business Media (www.springer.com)

Preface

The Transaction Processing Performance Council (TPC) is a non-profit organization established in August 1988. Over the years, the TPC has had a significant impact on the computing industry's use of industry-standard benchmarks. Vendors use TPC benchmarks to illustrate performance competitiveness for their existing products, and to improve and monitor the performance of their products under development. Many buyers use TPC benchmark results as points of comparison when purchasing new computing systems.

The information technology landscape is evolving at a rapid pace, challenging industry experts and researchers to develop innovative techniques for evaluation, measurement, and characterization of complex systems. The TPC remains committed to developing new benchmark standards to keep pace with these rapid changes in technology. One vehicle for achieving this objective is the TPC's sponsorship of the Technology Conference Series on Performance Evaluation and Benchmarking (TPCTC) established in 2009. With this conference series, the TPC encourages researchers and industry experts to present and debate novel ideas and methodologies in performance evaluation, measurement, and characterization.

The first TPC Technology Conference on Performance Evaluation and Benchmarking (TPCTC 2009) was held in conjunction with the 35th International Conference on Very Large Data Bases (VLDB 2009) in Lyon, France, during August 24–28, 2009.

The second TPC Technology Conference on Performance Evaluation and Benchmarking (TPCTC 2010) was held in conjunction with the 36th International Conference on Very Large Data Bases (VLDB 2010) in Singapore during September 13–17, 2010.

The third TPC Technology Conference on Performance Evaluation and Benchmarking (TPCTC 2011) was held in conjunction with the 37th International Conference on Very Large Data Bases (VLDB 2011) in Seattle, Washington, from August 29 to September 3, 2011.

The fourth TPC Technology Conference on Performance Evaluation and Benchmarking (TPCTC 2011) was held in conjunction with the 38th International Conference on Very Large Data Bases (VLDB 2012) in Istanbul, during August 27–31, 2012.

This book contains the proceedings of the fifth TPC Technology Conference on Performance Evaluation and Benchmarking (TPCTC 2013), held in conjunction with the 38th International Conference on Very Large Data Bases (VLDB 2013) held in Riva del Garda, Trento, Italy, during August 27–31, 2013, including seven selected peer-reviewed papers, a report from the TPC Public Relations committee (PR), and one invited paper.

The hard work and close cooperation of a number of people have contributed to the success of this conference. We would like to thank the members of TPC and the organizers of VLDB 2013 for their sponsorship, the members of the Program Committee and Publicity Committee for their support, and the authors and the participants, who are the primary reason for the success of this conference.

January 2014   Raghunath Nambiar
                                                                Meikel Poess

TPCTC 2013 Organization

General Chairs

Raghunath Nambiar   Cisco, USA
MeikelPoess   Oracle, USA

Program Committee

Alain Crolotte	Teradata, USA
Chaitanya Baru	San Diego Supercomputer Center, USA
Daniel Bowers	Gartner, USA
Marco Vieira	University of Coimbra, Portugal
Masaru Kitsuregawa	University of Tokyo, Japan
Michael Brey	Oracle, USA
TilmannRabl	University of Toronto, Canada
Xiaohua Tony Hu	Drexel University, USA
Wen Chen Hu	University of North Dakota, USA
Harumi Kuno	HP Labs, USA

Publicity Committee

Raghunath Nambiar	Cisco, USA
Andrew Bond	Red Hat, USA
Andrew Masland	NEC, USA
MeikelPoess	Oracle, USA
Reza Taheri	VMware, USA
Michael Majdalany	L&M Management Group, USA
Forrest Carman	Owen Media, USA
Andreas Hotea	Hotea Solutions, USA

Invited Speaker

Karl Huppler   IBM, USA

Keynote Speaker

Raghu Ramakrishnan   Microsoft, USA

About the TPC

Introduction to the TPC

The Transaction Processing Performance Council (TPC) is a non-profit organization that defines transaction processing and database benchmarks and distributes vendor-neutral performance data to industry. Additional information is available at http://www.tpc.org/.

TPC Memberships

Full Members

Full Members of the TPC participate in all aspects of the TPC's work, including development of benchmark standards and setting strategic direction.The Full Member application can be found at
http://www.tpc.org/information/about/app-member.asp.

Associate Members

Certain organizations may join the TPC as Associate Members. Associate Members may attend TPC meetings, but are not eligible to vote or hold office. Associate membership is available to non-profit organizations, educational institutions, market researchers, publishers, consultants, governments, and businesses that do not create, market, or sell computer products or services. The Associate Member application can be found at
http://www.tpc.org/information/about/app-assoc.asp.

Academic and Government Institutions

Academic and government institutions are invited join the TPC and a special invitation can be found at
http://www.tpc.org/information/specialinvitation.asp.

Contact the TPC

TPC
Presidio of San Francisco
Building 572B (surface)
P.O. Box 29920 (mail)
San Francisco, CA 94129-0920
Voice: 415-561-6272
Fax: 415-561-6120
Email: info@tpc.org

How to Order TPC Materials

All of our materials are now posted free of charge on our website. If you have any questions, please feel free to contact our office directly or by email at info@tpc.org

Benchmark Status Report

The TPC Benchmark Status Report is a digest of the activities of the TPC and its technical subcommittees. Sign-up information can be found at the following URL: http://www.tpc.org/information/about/email.asp.

TPC 2013 Organization

Full Members

Cisco
Dell
Fujitsu
HP
Hitachi
Huawei
IBM
Intel
Microsoft
NEC
Oracle
Redhat
Sybase (An SAP Company)
Teradata
Unisys
VMware

Associate Members

ITOM International Co
Gartner
San Diego Super Computing Center
Telecommunications Technology Association
University of Coimbra, Portugal

Steering Committee

Karl Huppler (IBM), Chair
Mike Brey (Oracle)
Charles Levine (Microsoft)
Raghunath Nambiar (Cisco)
Wayne Smith (Intel)

Public Relations Committee

Raghunath Nambiar (Cisco), Chair
Andrew Bond (Red Hat)

Andrew Masland(NEC)
MeikelPoess (Oracle)
Reza Taheri (VMware)

Technical Advisory Board

Jamie Reding (Microsoft), Chair
Andrew Bond (Red Hat)
Matthew Emmerton (IBM)
John Fowler (Oracle)
Bryon Georgson (HP)
Andrew Masland (NEC)
Wayne Smith (Intel)

Table of Contents

TPC State of the Council 2013

Raghunath Nambiar[1], Meikel Poess[2], Andrew Masland[3], H. Reza Taheri[4],
Andrew Bond[5], Forrest Carman[6], and Michael Majdalany[7]

[1] Cisco Systems, Inc., 3800 Zanker Road, San Jose, CA 95134, USA
rnambiar@cisco.com
[2] Oracle Corporation, 500 Oracle Pkwy, Redwood Shores, CA 94065, USA
meikel.poess@oracle.com
[3] NEC Corporation of America, 14335 NE 24th Street, Bellevue, WA 98007, USA
andy.masland@necam.com
[4] VMware, Inc., 3401 Hillview Ave, Palo Alto CA 94304, USA
rtaheri@vmware.com
[5] Red Hat, 100 East Davie Street, Raleigh, NC 27601, USA
abond@redhat.com
[6] Owen Media, 3130 E. Madison St., Suite 206, Seattle, WA 98112, USA
forrestc@owenmedia.com
[7] LoBue & Majdalany Mgmt Group, 572B Ruger St. San Francisco, CA 94129, USA
majdalany@lm-mgmt.com

Abstract. The TPC has played, and continues to play, a crucial role in providing the computer industry and its customers with relevant standards for total system performance, price-performance, and energy efficiency comparisons. Historically known for database-centric standards, the TPC is now developing benchmark standards for consolidation using virtualization technologies and multi-source data integration. The organization is also exploring new ideas such as Big Data and Big Data Analytics as well as an Express benchmark model to keep pace with rapidly changing industry demands. This paper gives a high level overview of the current state of the TPC in terms of existing standards, standards under development and future outlook.

Keywords: Industry Standard Benchmarks, Transaction Processing Performance Council.

1 TPC a Look Back and a Look Ahead

System benchmarks have played, and continue to play, a crucial role in the advancement of the computing industry. Existing system benchmarks are critical to both buyers and vendors. Buyers use benchmark results when evaluating new systems in terms of performance, price/performance, and energy efficiency, while vendors use benchmarks to demonstrate the competitiveness of their products and to monitor release-to-release progress of their products under development. With no standard system benchmarks available for Big Data systems, today's situation is similar to that of the mid-1980s, when the lack of standard database benchmarks led

R. Nambiar and M. Poess (Eds.): TPCTC 2013, LNCS 8391, pp. 1–15, 2014.
© Springer International Publishing Switzerland 2014

many system vendors to practice what is now referred to as "benchmarketing," a practice in which organizations make performance claims based on self-designed, highly biased benchmarks. The goal of publishing results from such tailored benchmarks was to state marketing claims, regardless of the absence of relevant and verifiable technical merit. In essence, these benchmarks were designed as forgone conclusions to fit a pre-established marketing message. Similarly, vendors would create configurations, referred to as "benchmark specials," that were specifically designed to maximize performance against a specific benchmark with limited benefit to real-world applications. The TPC was founded to address these issues and it continues to do so today. To keep up with rapid changes in the industry, the TPC introduced its annual international conference series on performance evaluation and benchmarking (TPCTC) in 2009.

2   TPC Benchmark Roadmap

Over the years, TPC benchmarks have raised the bar for what the computing industry has come to expect in terms of benchmarks themselves. Though the original focus has been on online transaction processing (OLTP) benchmarks, to-date the TPC has approved a total of nine independent benchmarks. Of these benchmarks, TPC-C, TPC-H, and TPC-E are currently active, and are widely being used by the industry.

TPC-V, TPC-VMC, and TPC-DI are under development. As described below, TPC-Express is another initiative from the TPC to bring out packaged benchmark kits that are easy to run and report.

The TPC-Pricing Specification and the TPC-Energy Specification are common across all the benchmark standards.

The timelines are shown in Figure 1.

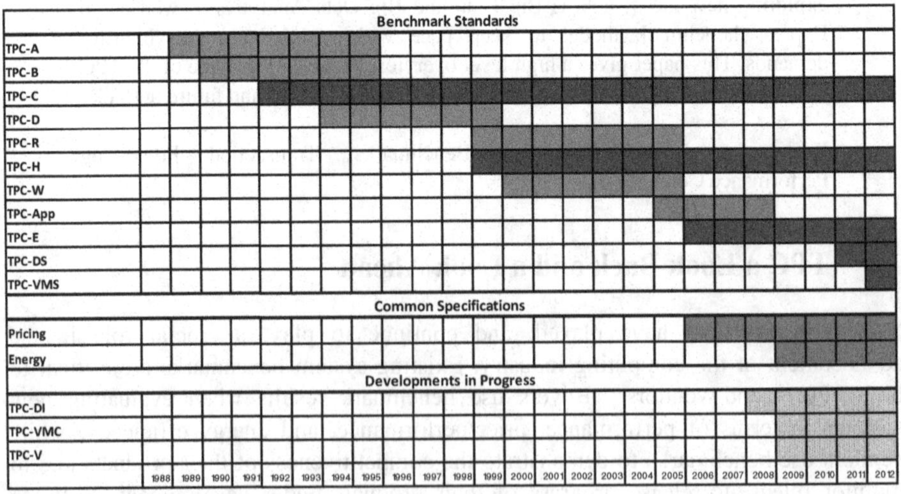

Fig. 1. TPC timeline (Color coding: blue=obsolete, red=current, green= common specifications, beige=under development)

3   TPC Development Status Report

3.1   TPC-Data Integration (TPC-DI)

Data Integration (DI), also known as "'ETL" (Extract, Transform, Load), is the analysis, combination, and transformation of data from a variety of data sources and formats into a unified data model representation. Having a performing data integration system is a key element of data warehousing, application integration, and business analytics solutions. This is especially important as the variety and volume of data are always increasing and performance of data integration systems is critical. Despite the significance of having a highly performing DI system, there has been no industry standard for measuring and comparing the performance of DI systems. Recognizing this benchmark void, the TPC established a subcommittee to develop TPC-DI, a benchmark for Data Integration. It is based on ideas first presented at TPCTC09. The release date of the benchmark is expected in 4th quarter 2013.

The TPC-DI benchmark workload transforms and combines data extracted from a fictitious On-Line Transaction Processing (OTLP) system and other data sources, and loads it into a data warehouse. The source and destination data models, data transformations, and implementation rules have been designed to be broadly representative of modern data integration requirements. No single benchmark can reflect the entire range of possible DI requirements. However, using data and operation models of a retail brokerage, it exercises a breadth of system components associated with DI environments, which are characterized by:

- The manipulation and loading of large volumes of data
- A mixture of transformation types including data validation, key lookups, conditional logic, data type conversions, aggregation operations, etc.
- Fact and dimensional table building and maintenance operations
- Multiple data sources having a variety of different data formats
- Historical loading and incremental updates of the destination data warehouse
- Consistency requirements ensuring that the integration process results in reliable and accurate data
- Multiple data tables with varied data types, attributes, and inter-table relationships

The benchmark is executed in a series of phases, consisting of:

- Initialization
- Loading the data warehouse with large volumes of historical data
- Two incremental updates to the data warehouse, each representing one day of new data
- An automated audit check to verify the results

The Performance Metric reported by TPC-DI is a throughput measure, the number of source rows processed per second. The metric combines the throughputs achieved for each phase to produce the single throughput performance metric.

3.2   TPC-Decision Support (TPC-DS)

The TPC Benchmark DS (TPC-DS) is a decision support benchmark that models several generally applicable aspects of a decision support system, including queries, and data maintenance. The benchmark provides a representative evaluation of the System Under Test's (SUT) performance as a general purpose decision support system.

This benchmark illustrates decision support systems that:

- Examine large volumes of data
- Give answers to real-world business questions
- Execute queries of various operational requirements and complexities (e.g., ad-hoc, reporting, iterative OLAP, data mining)
- Are characterized by high CPU and IO load
- Are synchronized with source OLTP databases through database maintenance functions that are executed while queries are being run, a.k.a. trickle updates

A benchmark result measures query throughput and data maintenance performance for a given hardware, operating system, and DBMS configuration under a controlled, complex, multi-user decision support workload. There have not been any benchmark publications since the benchmark was introduced and only one minor revision was published to clarify wording regarding trickle updates.

3.3   TPC -Virtualization in Progress

The TPC has been working on multiple fronts to deliver benchmarks for measuring the performance of virtualized databases. This section presents a benchmark that has already been released, one that is under development and close to being released, and one that is still a little further from completion.

3.3.1   TPC-VMS

Performance analysts have a choice of virtualization benchmarks [5], including some that have been around for years [6]. But TPC-VMS is the first industry standard virtualization benchmark with the characteristics that have made TPC benchmarks the benchmarks of choice for enterprise-class servers:

- Includes a Price/performance metric
- Is an audited benchmark
- Has database-centric workloads
- Scales the database size with performance when running TPC-E and TPC-C workloads

The goal of the TPC-VMS benchmark was to develop a benchmark specification quickly by utilizing the existing TPC benchmark specifications. The TPC Virtual Measurement Single System Specification (TPC-VMS) leverages the TPC-C, TPC-E, TPC-H, and TPC-DS benchmarks by adding the methodology and requirements for running and reporting performance metrics for virtualized databases. The intent of

TPC-VMS is to represent a virtualization environment where three database workloads are consolidated onto one server. Test sponsors choose one of the four benchmark workloads (TPC-C, TPC-E, TPC-H, or TPC-DS) and run one instance of that benchmark workload in each of the three virtual machines (VMs) on the system under test. The three virtualized databases must have the same attributes, e.g. the same number of TPC-C warehouses, the same number of TPC-E Load Units, or the same TPC-DS or TPC-H scale factors. The TPC-VMS Primary Performance Metric is the minimum value of the three TPC Benchmark Primary metrics for the TPC Benchmarks run in the Virtualization Environment.

Several characteristics of the benchmark are worth noting:

- It models a consolidation environment of three identical databases on three virtual machines with the same workload on the same OS, DBMS, etc.
- The four possible workloads are the well-understood existing TPC-C, TPC-E, TPC-H, and TPC-DS TPC benchmarks.
- To enhance ease of benchmarking for test sponsors, the benchmark was defined such that existing benchmarking kits for TPC-C, TPC-E, TPC-H, and TPC-DS can be used to also run the TPC-VMS variants of these workloads.
- An elegant feature of the benchmark is specifying that the metrics reported are those of the VM with the lowest primary performance metric. This avoids the possibility of a test sponsor *gaming* the test by dividing system resource unevenly among the VMs, but it does so without having to resort to complicated run rules to prevent such gaming.

The TPC-VMS benchmark was adopted in August of 2012, after a very short development phase of one year, hence meeting its goal of a quick development schedule. Prototyping results [7] show that the benchmark meets its goal of exercising the virtualization management system with a complex, database-centric workload.

3.3.2 TPC-V

In 2010, the TPC formed a subcommittee to develop a new benchmark for virtualized databases. The TPC-V benchmarks aims to capture some of the most important properties of databases in the cloud:

- Multiple VMs of varying sizes and different workload types.
- Load elasticity: the benchmark poses a challenge to the hypervisor to react to unexpected changes to the load, and allocate just the right amount of resources to each VM. TPC-V specifies four groups of VMs. Although a constant overall tpsV load level is maintained throughout the run time, the proportion directed to each group changes every twelve minutes, as depicted in the Figure 2 below.
- As the processing power of the system under test (SUT) grows, TPC-V specifies more sets of VMs in each of the four groups. The minimum configuration has four groups, one set per group, and three VMs per set for a total of twelve VMs. But unlike many other virtualization benchmarks, the number of sets does not scale linearly with the power of the SUT. Using a

logarithmic scale, TPC-V specifies two sets per group for today's high end systems, and around three sets per group for the high end systems of the foreseeable future. This makes sense in the context of databases in the cloud: a server may host hundreds of application VMs, but the number of database VMs on one server, even in a cloud environment, is likely to be much more limited.

- TPC-V uses the TPC-E DDL and DML as a starting point to reduce the development time. The TPC-V specification is vastly different from TPC-E, and comparing the results would bring to mind the proverbial apples and oranges comparison. Yet, the reliance on the proven properties of TPC-E has cut years from the TPC-V development process.

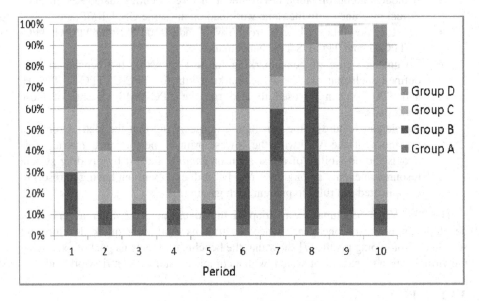

Fig. 2. Elastic load variation of TPC-V

Perhaps the most unique differentiator for TPC-V is that unlike previous TPC benchmarks, the TPC will provide a complete end-to-end, publicly available benchmarking kit along with the paper functional specification. The kit is written in Java and C++. The first implementation uses the open source PostgreSQL database. A full status update paper on TPC-V has been submitted to the TPCTC 2013.

3.3.3 TPC-VMC

TPC-VMS is the first virtualized database benchmark, and models consolidation. TPC-V takes that one step further by modeling heterogeneous workload types, varying load levels among the VMs, elasticity of load, and a VM count that scales with performance. But to truly model cloud environments, one has to include other properties such as:

- Multiple servers
- Load balancing among servers
- Migration of VMs between servers
- Deployment of VMs and applications

The TPC formed a working group to study the feasibility of such a benchmark [8]. The working group considered a number of proposals, and came up with the following requirements:

- The benchmark cannot become a test of *deep pockets*. In other words, if the number of servers is allowed to grow without bounds, a test sponsor can achieve any arbitrary performance level by simply assembling a configuration with just the right number of nodes. Note that this would be trivial for a benchmark such TPC-VMC since the application environment we are simulating is one of independent databases. So one can increase performance by simply adding more nodes. Surprisingly, one can use this very property to limit the number of servers in the configuration. A minimum set of servers can characterize the performance of a large number of servers in a large cloud environment. Therefore, the working group settled on no more than two or four servers.
- In keeping with the success of TPC-VMS in employing existing TPC benchmarking kits, the working group explored options that would not require modifications to existing kit.
- The benchmark proposal outlines a *choreographed* sequence of VM deployments and migrations, as depicted in Figure 3.

The working group has submitted its findings to the TPC, and is presently in hiatus. The TPC expects that once the TPC-V benchmark is released, the working group will resume and consider whether the TPC-V kit can be used to run a benchmark that includes migrations, deployment, etc. If the TPC-V kit proves to be well-received by the industry, extending it to simulate the properties required by TPC-VMC is only a small incremental step since the benchmark already deals with multiple VMs, elasticity, and load balancing within a server.

4   TPC-Express – A New Model for Benchmark Delivery

Traditionally, TPC benchmarks have been delivered in the form of a specification, allowing great flexibility in the way the benchmark application is implemented to satisfy the business case defined by the benchmark. This model worked well in times when customized application development was commonplace and when the various database products in the market delivered function in a wide variety of ways. The TPC considers this more traditional approach to its benchmarks as the "Enterprise" model. Compelling reasons to use the existing "Enterprise" benchmark model remain when the optimal application is developed to satisfy a functional specification.

Today, however, most database management products offer a suite of functions that are largely compatible for most database applications, and most commercial applications are purchased from an application provider. It makes good sense, then, to offer benchmarks that emulate these off-the-shelf products with the delivery of working benchmark applications in a downloadable benchmark kit, rather than requiring the development of the benchmark application by the implementer. This represents an exciting step for the TPC and those using TPC benchmarks. This new "Express" model will provide a kit that includes routines to build the database, run the benchmark application, report the results, and provide a level of validation for result compliance. This means that implementation of a benchmark can be accomplished much less expensively, with a higher confidence that the results are compliant and comparable.

A quick comparison of the two models is summarized in Table 1

Table 1. Express vs. Enterprise Models

	Express	Enterprise
Execution	Kit based (enhanced by specification)	Specification based (with some code)
Implementation	Out of the box	Customized
Audit Requirements	Mostly self validation	Full audit
Pricing	Not required	Required
ACID properties	ACI at most	Full ACID
Pricing model	License sales and benchmark registration	Benchmark registration
Expected volume	High	Limited
Cost to run the benchmark	Low	High
Time to run the benchmark	Short	Longer

Where the existing Enterprise benchmarks were typically only published by computer manufacturers, the TPC expects that the Express class of benchmarks will appeal to a wider audience that includes computer and software manufacturers, academic researchers as well as individuals interested in running test environment workloads to validate data center system changes.

The TPC is actively working to produce a first benchmark within the Express model. This will likely be a revision of an existing Enterprise benchmark, adjusted in ways to satisfy the needs of the Express model. The results will not be comparable with the parent Enterprise benchmark. In parallel, the TPC intends to produce a guide for other Express benchmark proposals that are both in the areas of traditional TPC benchmarks and in newer areas, such as database in the cloud, Big Data, Business Analytics, in-memory databases, and so on. The TPC welcomes proposals from within and outside of the TPC membership, and invites those who would like to participate in this development process to become active members.

5   TPC Technology Conference Series (TPCTC)

The information technology landscape is evolving at a rapid pace, challenging industry experts and researchers to develop innovative techniques for evaluation, measurement and characterization of complex systems. The TPC remains committed to developing new benchmark standards to keep pace, and one vehicle for achieving this objective is the sponsorship of the Technology Conference on Performance Evaluation and Benchmarking (TPCTC). Over the last four years we have held TPCTC successfully in conjunction with VLDB.

Table 2. TPCTC at a glance

TPCTC	VLDB	Location	Date	Keynote	Proceedings
TPCTC 2009	35th Int'l Conference	Lyon, France	August 24-28	Michael Stonebraker[1], M.I.T.	http://www.springer.com/978-3-642-10423-7
TPCTC 2010	36th Int'l Conference	Singapore	Septembe r 13-17	C. Mohan[2], IBM	http://www.springer.com/computer/com munication+networks/book/978-3-642-18205-1
TPCTC 2011	37th Int'l Conference	Seattle, WA	Aug 29 – Sep 3	Umesh Dayal[3], HP Labs	http://www.springer.com/computer/com munication+networks/book/978-3-642-32626-4
TPCTC 2012	38th Int'l Conference	Istanbul, Turkey	August 27-31	Michael Carey[4], UC Irvine	http://www.springer.com/computer/com munication+networks/book/978-3-642-36726-7
TPCTC 2013	39th Int'l Conference	Trento, Italy	August 26-30	Raghu Ramakrishnan[5], Microsoft	

The TPC Technology Conferences have had direct effect on the TPC's direction and activities:

- The formation of TPC's Virtualization working group (TPC-V) was a direct result of papers presented at TPCTC 2009. Proposals such as dependability aspects are under consideration for future benchmark enhancements.
- Several new benchmark ideas, enhancements to existing benchmarks and lessons learnt in practice were presented at TPCTC 2010 that had a direct

---

[1] Adjunct Professor, Massachusetts Institute of Technology, Cambridge, MA.
[2] IBM Fellow at the IBM Almaden Research Center, San Jose, CA.
[3] ACM Fellow and Chief Scientist of the Information Analytics Lab at HP Labs, Palo Alto, CA.
[4] Donald Bren Professor of Computer and Information Sciences, University of California, Irvine, CA.
[5] Technical Fellow, Microsoft, and Professor of Computer Sciences at the University of Wisconsin, Madison, WI.

impact to the TPC and the industry, e.g. a proposal for a generic data generator.

- Papers presented at TPCTC 2011 included new benchmark ideas in the area of Event Bases Systems, Mixed Workload Benchmarks, and Dependability Benchmarks. There were also various papers on enhancing existing TPC workloads, such as an enhancement to TPC-H and a dbgen implementation for TPC-H using the generic data generator PDGF. Some more theoretical papers included analytical models of benchmarks.
- Papers presented at TPCTC 2012 included new benchmark ideas in the area of big data, energy efficiency, Cloud, ETL, and virtualization.

With the 5th TPC Technology Conference on Performance Evaluation and Benchmarking (TPCTC 2013) proposal, the TPC strives to exceed the success of previous workshops by encouraging researchers and industry experts to present and debate novel ideas and methodologies in emerging performance evaluation and benchmarking areas. Authors are invited to submit original, unpublished papers that are not currently under review for any other conference or journal. The TPC also encourages the submission of extended abstracts, position statement papers and lessons learned in practice. The accepted papers will be published in the workshop proceedings, and selected papers will be considered for future TPC benchmark developments. Topics of interest include, but are not limited to:

- Big Data
- Cloud Computing
- Social media infrastructure
- Business intelligence
- Complex event processing
- Database optimizations
- Green computing
- Disaster tolerance and recovery
- Energy and space efficiency
- Hardware innovations
- Hybrid workloads
- Virtualization
- Lessons learned in practice using TPC workloads
- Enhancements to existing TPC workloads

6   Major Areas of Focus for 2014 and Beyond

6.1   Big Data

The last five years have seen a huge change in the industry landscape: Platforms that can handle Big Data workloads have become mainstream. Big Data refers to data sets that are too large and too complex to store and process in a cost effectively and timely manner using traditional tools like scale-up systems and relational management systems. Emerging from the Web 2.0 challenge, solutions are now available to provision and manage very large workloads, including Hadoop and NoSQL. Without doubt, enterprises see the value of Big Data and Big Data analytics across all major sectors, including health care, retail, education, and government, due to two main reasons. First is an increased number of people constantly connected to the internet and second there is an increased number of devices connected to the Internet. While there were 15 billion devices connected to the Internet in 2011 it is predicted that by year 2020 there will be 50 connected billion devices connected.

To face the challenges associated with the amount of data produced by the increased number of users and their devices, hardware and software infrastructure technologies have also evolved from traditional scale-up and client/server systems to massive scale-out clusters and clouds. Hadoop and NoSQL systems have become cost–effective, scalable platforms for handling massive amounts of structured, semi structured and unstructured data. Many of these technologies were a contribution of Web 2.0-era companies. Enterprises are also considering the use of Hadoop and NoSQL, realizing that storing and mining large data sets can help optimize their business processes, improve the customer experience, uncover strategic and competitive opportunities, and thereby gain a competitive advantage. With this new Big Data landscape, and multiple technologies to choose from, there is a need for industry standards so users can see fair and unbiased comparisons of technologies and solutions.

With no standard system benchmarks available for Big Data systems, today's situation is similar to that of the middle 1980s, when the lack of standard database benchmarks led many system vendors to practice what is now referred to as "benchmarketing," a practice in which organizations make performance claims based on self-designed, highly biased benchmarks.

Some of the existing TPC benchmarks like TPC-H and TPC-DS can easily be extended for use in large structured datasets. For example, current TPC-H and TPC-Ds benchmarks support scale factors of 100GB, 300B, 1TB, 3TB, 10TB and 30TB. This can be extended to larger scale factors like 100TB, 300GB, 1TB, 3PB and more, following the log scale, using existing data generation tools and queries. There is work in progress to extend TPC-DS to handle unstructured data also. There are initiatives like WBDB (Workshop on Big Data Benchmarking), which is intended developed brand new workloads. TPC-H and TPC-DS contain a diverse set of structured data, which makes them a suitable candidate for a Big Data benchmark.

As reported in Big Data Management, Technologies, and Applications, one of the outcomes of the first workshop on Big Data Benchmarking is BigBench _Ref355098135. BigBench is an end-to-end, Big Data benchmark proposal. It is based on TPC-DS. Hence, its underlying business model is a product retailer. In addition to TPC-DS, it proposes a data model and synthetic data generator that address the variety, velocity and volume aspects of Big Data systems containing structured, semi-structured, and unstructured data. The structured part of BigBench's data model is adopted from TPC-DS. It is enriched with semi-structured and unstructured data components. The semi-structured part captures registered and guest user clicks on the retailer's web site. The unstructured data captures product reviews submitted online.

The data generator, which was designed for BigBench, provides scalable volumes of raw data based on a scale factor. BigBench's workload is designed around a set of queries against the data model. From a business prospective, the queries cover the different categories of Big Data analytics proposed by McKinsey. From a technical prospective, the queries are designed to span three different dimensions based on data sources, query processing types and analytic techniques. In the SIGMOD paper, the authors further illustrate the feasibility of BigBench by presenting an implementation on Teradata's Aster Database. The test includes generating and loading a 200 Gigabyte BigBench data set and testing the workload by executing the BigBench queries (written using Teradata Aster SQL-MR) and reporting their response times.

BigBench's data model focuses on volume, variety, and velocity. The variety property of BigBench is illustrated in Figure 4. The structured portion of BigBench's data model is adapted directly from TPC-DS' data model, which also depicts a product retailer _Ref355098116 [13]. BigBench adds a table for prices from the retailer's competitors to the portion of TPC-DS that contain store and online sales data. TPC-DS structured part is enriched with semi-structured and un-structured data shown in the lower and right hand side of Figure 4. The semi-structured part is composed by clicks made by customers and guest users visiting the retailer's web site. The design assumes the semi-structured data to be in a key-value format similar to Apache's web server log format. The un-structured data in the new model is covered by product reviews that can be submitted by guest users or actual customers.

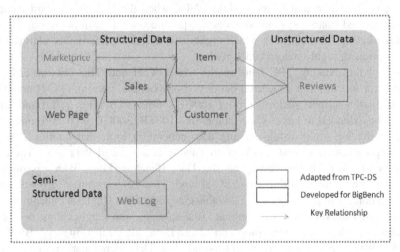

Fig. 4. Logical Data Model BigBench (Adapted from   _Ref355098135)

6.2   OpenStack

The term cloud computing has different meanings depending on the target environment. There are three main types of services provided by cloud environments:

Infrastructure-as-a-Service (IaaS), Platform-as-a-Service (PaaS), and Software-as-a-Service (SaaS). The difference between these various cloud environments has mostly to do with how much of the solution stack the user can control. For instance, with SaaS the user has access to a piece of software running in the cloud but has no control over what operating system it is running on whereas in IaaS the user has control over many aspects of the solution stack.

OpenStack (www.openstack.org) is an open source project to define and build a highly scalable common cloud computing platform for public and private clouds. OpenStack would be defined as an IaaS cloud service. Over 150 companies are participating in some aspect of the OpenStack development effort, including many of the TPC member companies.

The OpenStack project has an extremely active development community. The first OpenStack release was in October of 2010, and there have been six releases over the course of the following two and a half years. With two to three releases a year, the pace of development is very rapid. This fast development cadence is necessary, since many vendors want to implement cloud environments starting immediately rather than some time in the future.

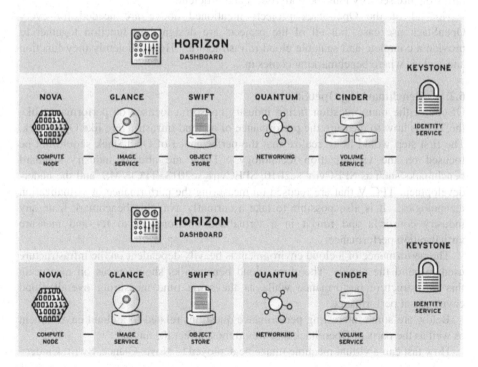

Fig. 5. OpenStack Architecture (http://www.redhat.com/products/cloud-computing/openstack/)

The design of OpenStack contains components in the areas of compute, networking, and storage. The parts of OpenStack that deal with the compute aspect of a cloud have project names such as Nova, Glance, and Horizon. Nova is a framework for providing virtual servers on demand in an OpenStack environment. Nova does not provide virtualization functionality, but can be hooked into various virtualization technologies via an API. Glance provides a way to create a catalog of virtual disk images for the compute framework to reference and use. Horizon will be the most recognizable part of OpenStack to users since it is the GUI management interface for OpenStack.

The network and storage area is addressed by the Quantum, Swift, and Cinder projects. Quantum provides network connectivity as a service and interfaces with many different types of networking technologies. The Swift and Cinder projects both deal with storage, but different aspects of storage. Swift provides for object storage, while Cinder can provide persistent block storage to the virtual machines deployed in OpenStack.

A key aspect to any cloud environment is security. In the OpenStack environment authentication and authorization are handled by the Keystone project. Cloud infrastructure security must be both robust and efficient.

Not all of the OpenStack projects mentioned above are needed for every OpenStack use case, but all of the projects are designed to function together to provide a complete and scalable cloud infrastructure. How efficiently they function and scale is where benchmarking comes in.

6.2.1   Benchmarking OpenStack

Of course the main question facing industry consortia focused on performance like the TPC is how to measure the performance of a cloud infrastructure like OpenStack. The first step would be to realize that the performance of OpenStack should not be focused on the virtualization technology. There are already industry standard benchmarks such as SPECvirt_sc2010, SPECvirt_sc2013, TPC-VMS, and the under-development TPC-V that are focused on measuring the performance of virtualization technologies. It is also possible to take a currently available benchmark from any industry consortia and run it in a virtualized environment to try and measure virtualization performance.

The performance of a cloud environment is heavily dependent on the infrastructure used to build the cloud. Therefore, cloud benchmarks should focus on measuring this infrastructure performance while as the same time measuring overall cloud environment performance.

Below are some interesting performance questions related to a cloud environment as well as the parts of OpenStack that would most affect the answer.

How fast can a virtual machine image be deployed? Nova, Glance, Swift, Cinder

- Do my tasks take longer to run in a cloud than if I was just using virtualization? Nova, Glance, Quantum, Swift, Cinder
- What kind of performance slowdown does the security of the cloud cause? Nova, Keystone

- Do the answers to any of the previous questions change as the cloud environment scales?   All OpenStack projects

The use of a cloud environment for providing compute resources to a specific set of customers revolves mainly around the ability to meet particular response time criteria for those customers.   If a cloud environment cannot meet a customer's response time needs then dedicated hardware would have to be deployed instead. Therefore, any cloud benchmark must be designed around response time requirements and have it built into every aspect of the benchmark.

Because there are many different aspects to a cloud infrastructure like OpenStack, a benchmark designed to test such an environment would have to have many aspects as well.   Potentially a suite of tests will be required with each designed to put stress on a particular aspect of the OpenStack environment to see how it performs.   The challenge to having a benchmark that is made up of multiple tests is normalizing multiple data points into a single metric score.   For an industry standard benchmark to be successful, one main metric is ideal.   Multiple secondary metrics could be defined, but they should be rolled up into a single main metric.

7   Conclusion

In an environment of rapid and pervasive change, the TPC remains committed to serve the industry with benchmark standards that are relevant and up to date. While the TPC's traditional, Enterprise benchmarks continue to be the gold-standard for large database workloads, the organization has several new benchmarks in process. TPC-DI, TPC-V, and the new TPC-Express model are such initiatives that cover workloads as diverse as data integration, virtualization, and an entire new approach to benchmarks The TPC is also exploring ideas and methodologies to create benchmarks for Big Data and OpenStack. The organization also strongly supports benchmarking innovation through the TPC Technical Conference (TPCTC) and looks forward to incorporating innovative ideas from the 5th TPCTC.

Acknowledgements. The authors thank the past and present members of the TPC for their contribution to the specifications and documents referenced in this paper.

References

1. Nambiar, R., Poess, M. (eds.): TPCTC 2012. LNCS, vol. 7755. Springer, Heidelberg (2013)
2. Nambiar, R., Poess, M. (eds.): TPCTC 2011. LNCS, vol. 7144. Springer, Heidelberg (2012)
3. Nambiar, R., Poess, M. (eds.): TPCTC 2010. LNCS, vol. 6417. Springer, Heidelberg (2011)
4. Nambiar, R., Poess, M. (eds.): TPCTC 2009. LNCS, vol. 5895. Springer, Heidelberg (2009)
5. SPEC Virtualization Committee: http://www.spec.org/virt_sc2010/, http://www.spec.org/virt_sc2013/
6. VMware, Inc., http://www.vmware.com/products/vmmark/overview.html
7. Smith, W.D., Sebastian, S.: Virtualization Performance Insights from TPC-VMS, http://www.tpc.org/tpcvms/tpc-vms-2013-1.0.pdf
8. Smith, W.D.: Characterizing Cloud Performance with TPC Benchmarks. In: Nambiar, R., Poess, M. (eds.) TPCTC 2012. LNCS, vol. 7755, pp. 189–196. Springer, Heidelberg (2013)

TPC-BiH: A Benchmark for Bitemporal Databases

Martin Kaufmann[1,2], Peter M. Fischer[3], Norman May[1],
Andreas Tonder[1], and Donald Kossmann[2]

[1] SAP AG, 69190 Walldorf, Germany
{norman.may,andreas.tonder}@sap.com
[2] ETH Zurich, 8092 Zurich, Switzerland
{martin.kaufmann,donald.kossmann}@inf.ethz.ch
[3] Albert-Ludwigs-Universität, Freiburg, Germany
peter.fischer@cs.uni-freiburg.de

Abstract. An increasing number of applications such as risk evaluation in banking or inventory management require support for temporal
data. After more than a decade of standstill, the recent adoption of some
bitemporal features in SQL:2011 has reinvigorated the support among
commercial database vendors, who incorporate an increasing number of
relevant bitemporal features. Naturally, assessing the performance and
scalability of temporal data storage and operations is of great concern
for potential users. The cost of keeping and querying history with novel
operations (such as time travel, temporal joins or temporal aggregations)
is not adequately reflected in any existing benchmark. In this paper, we
present a benchmark proposal which provides comprehensive coverage
of the bitemporal data management. It builds on the solid foundations
of TPC-H but extends it with a rich set of queries and update scenarios. This workload stems both from real-life temporal applications from
SAP's customer base and a systematic coverage of temporal operators
proposed in the academic literature. We present preliminary results of
our benchmark on a number of temporal database systems, also highlighting the need for certain language extensions.

Keywords: Bitemporal Databases, Benchmark, Data Generator.

1 Introduction

Temporal information is widely used in real-world database applications, e.g.,
to plan for the delivery of a product or to record the time a state of an order
changed. Particularly the need for tracing and auditing the changes made to a
data set and the ability to make decisions based on past or future assumptions are
important use cases for temporal data. As a consequence, temporal features were
included into the SQL:2011 standard [9], and an increasing number of database
systems offer temporal features, e.g., Oracle, DB2, SAP HANA, or Teradata. As
temporal data is often stored in an append-only mode, temporal tables quickly
grow very large. This makes temporal processing a performance-critical aspect

R. Nambiar and M. Poess (Eds.): TPCTC 2013, LNCS 8391, pp. 16–31, 2014.

of many analysis tasks. Clearly, an understanding of the performance character-istics of different implementations of temporal queries is required to select the most appropriate database system for the desired workload. Unfortunately, at this time there is no generally accepted benchmark for temporal workloads.

For non-temporal data the TPC has defined TPC-H and TPC-DS for an-alytical tasks and TPC-C and TPC-E for transactional workloads. Especially TPC-H and TPC-C are popular for comparing database systems. These bench-marks query only the most recent version of the data. We propose to leverage the insights gained with TPC-H and to TPC-C while widening the scope for temporal data. In particular, it should be possible to evaluate all TPC-H queries at different system times. This allows us to compare results on temporal data with those on non-temporal data. We carefully introduce additional parameters to examine the temporal dimension. Furthermore, we propose additional queries that resemble typical use cases we encountered in real-world use cases at SAP but also during literature review. In some cases, the expressiveness of SQL:2011 is not sufficient to express these queries in a succinct way. For example, the sim-ulation of temporal aggregation in SQL:2011 results in rather complex queries.

More precisely, we propose a novel benchmark for temporal queries which are based on real-world use cases. As such, these queries retrieve both previous states of the system (i.e., a certain system time) but they also examine time intervals defined in the business domain (i.e., application time); this concept was introduced as the bitemporal data model by Snodgrass [12]. The benchmark we propose contains a data generator which first generates a TPC-H data set extended with some temporal data. In contrast to previous related work (such as [1] and [2]) it also generates a history of values using various business transactions on this data to generate system times. These transactions are inspired by the TPC-C benchmark, and they are designed to keep the characteristics generated by TPC-H dbgen at every point in time. Consequently, all TPC-H queries can be executed on the generated data, and their result properties for certain system times are comparable to those in the standard TPC-H benchmark. However, over time the overall data set grows as the previous versions are preserved in order to support time travel to a previous state of the system. In order to evaluate the time dimension, for this benchmark, we define additional queries which retrieve data at different points in time.

The remainder of this paper is structured as follows: In Section 2 we summa-rize the design goals for our proposed benchmark TPC-BiH. We survey related work on benchmarking temporal databases in Section 3. In the core part of the paper (Section 4), we define the schema, the data generator for temporal data, and the queries comprising the benchmark. We analyze two systems that support temporal queries, and we present performance measurements for our benchmark (Section 5). In Section 6, we summarize our findings and point out future work.

2   Goals and Methodology

The goal of this paper is to present a comprehensive benchmark for bitemporal query processing. This benchmark includes all necessary definitions as well as the relevant tools such as data generators. The benchmark setting reflects real-life customer workloads (which have typically not been formalized to match the current expression of the bitemporal model) and is complemented by synthetic queries to test certain operations. The benchmark is targeted towards SQL:2011, which has recently adopted core parts of the temporal data model. Since the expressiveness of SQL:2011 is limited (no complex temporal join, no temporal aggregation), we provide alternative versions of the queries using language extensions. Similarly, in order to support DBMS's which provide temporal support, but have not (yet) adopted SQL:2011 (like Oracle or Teradata), we provide alternative queries.

The schema builds on a well-understood existing non-temporal analytics benchmark: TPC-H. Its tables are extended with different types of history classes, such as degenerated, fully bitemporal or multiple user times. The benchmark data is designed to provide a range of different temporal update patterns, varying the ratio of history vs. initial data, the types of operations (UPDATE, INSERT and DELETE) as well as the temporal distributions within and between the temporal dimensions. The data distributions and correlations stay stable with regard to system time updates and evolve according to well-defined update scenarios in the application time domain. The data generator we developed can be scaled in the dimensions of initial data size and history length independently, providing support for many different scenarios.

Our query workload provides a coverage of common temporal DB requirements. It covers operations such as *time travel, key in time, temporal joins*, and *temporal aggregations* – the latter is not directly expressible in SQL:2011. Similarly, we investigate many patterns of storage access and time- vs. key-oriented access with varying ranges and selectivity. The query workload also covers the different temporal dimensions (system and application time): The focus of the queries is on stressing the system for individual time dimensions while considering correlations among the dimensions whenever relevant.

In summary, our benchmark fulfills the requirements mentioned in the benchmark handbook by Jim Gray [3], i.e., it is

- *relevant*, since it covers all typical temporal operations.
- *portable*, since it targets SQL:2011 and provides extensions for systems not completely supporting SQL:2011.
- *scalable*, since it provides well-defined data which can be generated in different sizes for base data and history.
- *understandable*, since all queries have a meaning in application scenarios and in terms of operator/system "stress".

3   Related Work on Temporal Benchmarks

The foundation of the bitemporal data model was established in the proposal for TSQL2 [12]. For a single row the system time – in the original paper called *transaction time* – defines different versions as they were created by DML statements on a row. The system time is immutable, and the values are implicitly generated during transaction commit. Orthogonal to that, validity intervals can be defined on the application level – called *valid time* in the original paper. An example is the specification of the visibility of some marketing campaigns to users. Unlike the system time, the application time can be updated, and both interval boundaries may refer to times in the past, present, or future. The concept of the bitemporal model is now also applied in the SQL:2011 standard [9]. This standard focuses on basic operations like time travel on a single table. Complex temporal joins or aggregations are out of scope, but they are acknowledged as relevant scenarios for future versions of the SQL standard.

The benchmarks published by the TPC are the most commonly used benchmarks for databases. While these benchmarks used to focus either on analytical or transactional workloads, recently a combination has been proposed: The CH-benCHmark [2] extends the TPC-C schema by adding three tables from the TPC-H schema. Yet, no time dimension is included in these benchmarks.

Benchmarking the temporal dimension has been the focus of several studies: In 1995, a research proposal by Dunham et al. outlined possible directions and requirements for such a benchmark. The approach for building a temporal benchmark and the query classes come close to our methods.

A later work by Kuala and Robertson [5] provides logical models of several temporal database application areas alongside with queries expressed in an informal manner. The test suite of temporal database queries [4] from the TSQL2 editors provides a large number of temporal queries focused on functional testing rather than performance evaluation.

A study on spatio-temporal databases by Werstein [13] evaluates existing benchmarks and concludes that the temporal aspects of these benchmarks are insufficient. In turn, a number of queries are informally defined to overcome this limitation.

The work that is most closely related to ours was presented at TPCTC 2012 and includes a proposal to add a temporal dimension to the TPC-H Benchmark [1]. The authors also use TPC-H as a starting point, extend some tables with temporal columns to express bitemporal data, and rely on the data generator and the original queries of TPC-H as part of their workload. Yet, this work seems to be more focused on sketching the possibilities for the bitemporal data model rather than providing explicit definitions of data and queries. Specific differences exist in the language used (we focus on SQL:2011, in [1] a variant of TSQL2 is applied) as well as the derivation of application timestamps (we use existing temporal information in TPC-H for the initial version). Our update scenarios and queries cover a broader range of cases and aim to provide more properties on data and queries.

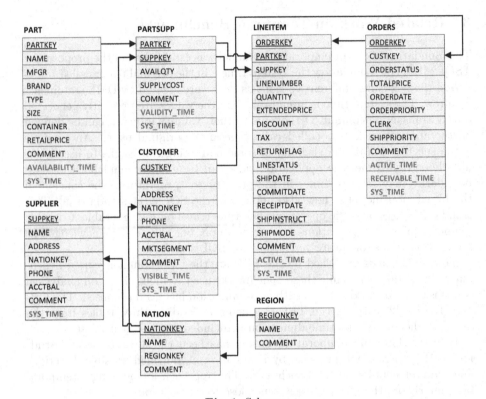

Fig. 1. Schema

4   Definition of the TPC-BiH Benchmark

The definition of our benchmark consists of a schema, properties of the benchmark data and a range of queries. Our benchmark mainly targets the current
SQL:2011 standard, but we also show examples how it can be translated to a
system with other temporal expressions.

Showing the full SQL code for all statements and queries is not possible due
to the space constraints of a workshop paper. Thus, we describe representative
examples in this paper and refer to a technical report [7] which includes all
queries and definitions in detail.

4.1   Schema

The schema we use in our benchmark is shown in Figure 1. As stated before, it
is based on the TPC-H schema and adds temporal columns in order to express
system and application times. Each of these time dimensions is stored as an
interval and represented physically as two columns, e.g., sys_time_begin and
sys_time_end. This means that any query defined on the TPC-H schema can run
on our data set, and will give meaningful results, reflecting the current system

time and the full range of application time versions. Specific other temporal dimensions can be added in a fairly straightforward manner. The additional temporal columns are chosen in such a way that the schema contains tables with different temporal properties: Some tables are kept unversioned, some express a correlated/degenerated behavior. Most tables are fully bitemporal, and we also consider the case in which a table has multiple "user" times. Even if the latter is not well specified in the standard, we observe it a lot in customer use cases.

More specifically, we do not add any temporal columns to REGION and NATION. This is also plausible from application semantics, since this kind of information rarely ever changes. All other relations at least include a system time dimension. For SUPPLIER we simulate a degenerated table by only giving a system time. Since this single time dimension is determined by the loading/updating timing, we do not use any temporal correlation queries between this table and truly bi-dimensional tables. For all the remaining relations, we determine the application time from the existing information present in the data: Tuples in LINEITEM are valid as long as any operation like shipping them is pending. Likewise, tuples from PART are valid when they can be ordered, tuples from CUSTOMER when the customer is visible to the system, tuples from PART-SUPP when the price and the amount are valid. Finally, ORDERS has two time dimensions: $ACTIVE\_TIME$: when was the order "active" (i.e., placed, but not delivered yet) and $RECEIVABLE\_TIME$: when the bill for the order can be paid (i.e., invoice sent to customer, but not paid yet). Both application times become part of the schema. Since current DBMSs only support a single application time, we designate $ACTIVE\_TIME$ as such, and keep $RECEIVABLE\_TIME$ as a "regular" timestamp column. Likewise, if a DBMS does not provide any support for application time, application times are mapped to normal timestamp columns.

4.2   Benchmark Data

Complementing TPC-H with an extensive update workload has been proposed before. Given the structural similarity and the wide recognition, TPC-C has been used for this purpose, e.g., in [2]. We also used a similar approach (with additional timestamp assignment) in a previous version of the benchmark [8], but this proved to not be fully adequate: The set of update scenarios is quite small, and does not provide much emphasis on temporal aspects such as timestamp correlations. The query mix also constrains the flexibility in terms of temporal properties, e.g., since a fixed ratio of updates needs to go to specific tables.

The standard TPC-H has only a very limited number of "refresh" queries, which furthermore do not contain any updates to values. Nonetheless, the data produced by the data generator serves a good "initial" data set. The application time columns defined in the schema are initialized with the temporal data already present in this data: Extreme values of shipdate, commitdate and receiptdate define the validity interval of LINEITEM. Given the dependencies among the data items (e.g., LINEITMES in an ORDER), we can now derive plausible application times for all bitemporal tables. Where needed, we complement this information with random distributions. The resulting data will contain data tuples with "open" time intervals, since customers or parts may have a validity far into the future.

To express the evolution of data, we define nine update scenarios, stressing different aspects among tables, values, and times:

1. *New Order*: Choose or create a customer, choose items and create an order on them.
2. *Cancel Order*: Remove an order, its dependent lineitems and adapt the number of available parts
3. *Deliver Order*: Update the order status and the lineitem status, adapt the available parts and the customer's balance.
4. *Receive Payment*: Update currently pending orders and the related customers' balances.
5. *Update Stock*: Increase available parts of a supplier.
6. *Delay Availability*: Postpone the date after which items are available from a supplier to a later date, e.g., due to a shipping backlog.
7. *Price Change*: Adapt the price of parts, choosing times from a range spanning from past to future application time.
8. *Update Supplier*: Update the supplier balance. This update stresses a degenerated table.
9. *Manipulate Order Data*: Choose an "old" order (with the application time far before system time) and update its price. This update changes values while keeping the application times (i.e., trying to hide this change).

Since the initial data generation and the data evolution mix are modeled independently, we can control the size of the initial data (called h like in TPC-H) and the length of the history (called m) separately, thus permitting cases like large initial data with a short history ($h \gg m$), small initial data with a long history ($h \ll m$) or any other combination. Similarly to the scaling settings in TPC-H, where $h = 1.0$ corresponds to 1 GB of data, we normalize $m = 1.0$ to the same size, and use the same (linear) scaling rules.

Table 1 describes the outcome of applying a mix of these queries on the various tables. The history growth ratio describes how many update operations per initial tuple happen when $h = m$. As we can see, CUSTOMER and SUPPLIER get a fairly high number of history entries per tuple, while ORDERS and LINEITEM see proportionally fewer history operations. When taking the sizes of the initial relations into account, the bulk of history operations is still performed on LINEITEM and ORDER. A second aspect on which the tables differ is the kind of history operations: SUPPLIER, CUSTOMER and PARTSUPP only receive **UPDATE** statements, whereas the remaining bitemporal relations will see a mix of operations. LINEITEM is strongly dominated by **INSERT** operations ($>$ 60 percent), ORDERS less so (50 percent inserts and 42 percent updates). CUSTOMERS in turn see mostly **UPDATE** operations ($>$ 70 percent). The temporal specialization follows the specification in the schema, providing SUPPLIER as a degenerate table. Finally, existing application time periods can be overwritten with new values for CUSTOMER, PART, PARTSUPP and ORDERS which

Table 1. Properties of the History for each Table

Table	History growth ratio	Dominant Operations	Temporal Specialization	Overwrite App.Time
NATION	None	None	non-versioned	no
REGION	None	None	non-versioned	no
SUPPLIER	5	Update	degenerate	no
CUSTOMER	3.7	Update	fully bitemporal	yes
PART	0.25	Update	fully bitemporal	yes
PARTSUPP	0.72	Update	fully bitemporal	yes
LINEITEM	0.32	Insert	fully bitemporall	no
ORDER	0.4	Insert	fully bitemporal	yes

refers to the use case of updating application time, which is an important feature of the bitemporal data model.

We implemented a generator to derive the application times from the TPC-H dbgen output for the initial version and generate the data evolution mix. The generator accounts for the different ways temporal data is supported by current temporal DBMS. Initial evaluations show that this generator can generate 0.6 Million tuples/sec, compared to 1.7 Million tuples/sec of dbgen on the same machine. The data generator can also be configured to compute a data set consisting purely of tuples that are valid at the end of the generation interval. This is useful when comparing the cost of temporal data management on the latest version against a non-temporal database.

4.3   Queries

Given the multi-dimensional space of possible temporal query classification, we cluster the queries among common dimensions: Data access [10], temporal operators and specific temporal correlations.

Pure-Timeslice Queries (Time Travel). The first group of queries is concerned with testing "slices" of time, i.e., establishing the state concerning a specific time for a table or a set of tables. Also known as *Time Travel*, this is the most commonly supported and used class of temporal queries. Given that time in a bitemporal database has more than one dimension, one can specify different slicing options for each of these dimensions: Each dimension could be treated as a point or as complete slice, e.g., fixing the application time to June 1st, 2013, while considering the full evolution through system time. Further aspects to study are the combination of time travel operations (e.g., to compare values at different points in time), implicit vs. explicit expressions for time and the impact of underlying data/temporal update patterns. The first set of queries is targeted for testing various aspect of time travel in isolation, consisting of nine queries with variants.

T1 and T2 are our baseline queries, performing a point-point access for both temporal dimensions. By varying both timestamps accordingly, particular combinations can easily be specified, e.g., tomorrow's state in application time, as recorded yesterday. The difference between T1 and T2 is according to the underlying data: T1 uses CUSTOMER, a table with many update operations and large history, but stable cardinalities. T2, in turn, uses ORDERS, a table with

a generally smaller history and a focus on insertions. This way, we can study
the cost of time travel operations on significantly different histories. T3 and T4
correlate data from two time travel operations within the same table. Comparing their results with T2 (very selective) and T5 (entire history) gives an insight
into whether any sharing of history operations is possible. T4 adds a TOP N
condition, providing possible room for optimization in the database system. T5
retrieves the complete history of the ORDERS table. Given that all data is requested, it should serve as a yardstick for the maximal cost of simple time travel
operations. T6 performs temporal slicing, i.e., retrieving all data of one temporal dimension, while keeping the other to a point. This provides insights if the
DBMS prefers any dimension, and a comparison of T2 and T5 yields insights
if any optimization for points vs. slices are available. T7 complements T6 by
implicitly specifying current system time, providing an understanding as to if
different approaches of specifying current time work equally well. T8 and T9 investigate the behavior of additional application times, as outlined in Section 4.1.
Since the standard currently only allows a single, designated application time, we
can study the benefits of explicit vs. implicit application times. In that context,
T8 uses point data (like T2), while T9 uses slicing (like T6).

The second set of timeslice queries focuses on application-oriented workloads,
providing insights on how well synthetic time travel performance translates into
complex analytical queries, e.g., accounting for additional data access cost and
possibly disabled optimizations. For this purpose, we use the 22 standard TPC-H
queries (similar to what [1] proposes) and extend them to allow the specification
of both a system and an application time point. Possible evaluations might
contain determining the cost of accessing the current version (in both system
as well as current application time) compared against the logically same data
stored in a non-temporal table (see Section 4.2).

Pure-Key Queries (Audit). The next class of queries we study poses an orthogonal problem: Instead of retrieving all tuples for a particular point in time,
we process the history of a specific tuple or a small set of tuples. This way, we
can investigate how tuples evolve over time, e.g., for auditing or trend detection. This evolution can be considered along the system time, the application
time(s) or both. Additional aspects to study are the effects of constraints on
the version range (complete time range, some time period, some versions) and
type of tuple selection, e.g., keys or predicates. In total, we specify 6 queries,
each with small variants to account for the different time dimensions: K1 selects
the tuple using a primary key, returns many columns and does not place any
constraints on the temporal range. For key-based histories, this should provide
the yardstick, and also offers clear insights into the organization of the storage of
temporal data. The cost of this operation can also be compared against T5 and
T6, which retrieve all versions of all tuples (for both dimensions or each time
dimension, each). To allow easy comparison with the T queries, all queries are
executed on the ORDERS relation. K2 alters K1 by placing a constraint on the
temporal range. Compared to K1, this additional information should provide an
optimization possibility. K3 alters K2 even further by only retrieving a single

column, providing optimization potential for decomposition or column stores. K4 complements K2 by constraining not the temporal range (by a time interval), but the number of versions (by using TOP N). While the intent is quite similar to K2, the semantics and possible execution strategies are quite different. K5 constitutes a special case of K4 in which only the immediately preceding version is retrieved, employing no TOP N expression, but a timestamp correlation. From a technical point of view, this provides additional potential for optimization. From a language point of view, such an access is required for queries that perform change detection. K6 chooses the tuples not via a key of the underlying table, but using a range predicate on a value (o_totalprice). Besides a general comparison to key-based access, choosing the value of this parameters allows us to study the impact of the selectivity on the computation cost.

Range-Timeslice Queries. As the most general access pattern, range-timeslice queries permit any combination of constraints on both value and temporal aspects. As a result, a broad range of queries falls into that range. We will provide a set of application-derived workloads here, highlighting the variety and the different challenges it brings. As before, these queries contain variants which restrict one time dimension to a point, while varying the other.

R1 considers state change modeling by querying those customers who moved to the US at a particular point in time and still live there. The SQL expression involves two temporal evaluations on the same relation and a join of the results. R2 also handles state modeling, but instead of detecting changes, it computes state durations for LINEITEMs (the shipping time). Compared to R1, the intermediate results are much bigger, but no temporal filters are applied when combining them. R3 expresses temporal aggregation, i.e., computing aggregates for each version or time range of the database. At SAP, this turned out to be one of the most sought-after analyses of temporal data. However, SQL:2011 does not provide much support for this use case. The first query (R3.a) computes the greatest number of unshipped items in a time range. In SQL:2011, this requires a rather complex and costly join over the time interval boundaries to determine change points, followed by a grouping on these boundaries for the aggregates. The second query (R3.b) computes the maximum value of unshipped orders within one year. As before, interval joins and grouping are required. R4 computes the products with the smallest difference in stock levels over the history. While the temporal semantics are rather easy to express, the same tables need to be accessed multiple times, and significant amount of post-processing is required. R5 covers temporal joins by computing how often a customer had a balance of less than 5000 while also having orders with a price greater than 10. The join therefore not only includes value join criteria (on the respective keys), but also time correlation. R7 computes changes between versions over a full set, retrieving those suppliers who increased their prices by more than 7.5 percent in a single update. R7 thus generalizes K4/K5 by determining previous versions for all keys, not just specific ones.

Bitemporal Queries. Nearly all queries so far have treated the two temporal dimensions in the same way: Keeping one dimension fixed, while performing different operations types of operations on the other. While this is a fairly
common pattern in real-life queries, we also want to gain a more thorough understanding of queries stressing both time dimensions. Snodgrass [11] provides
a classification of bitemporal queries. Our first set of bitemporal queries follows
this approach and creates complementary query variants to cover all relevant
combinations. These variants span both time dimensions and vary the usage of
each time dimension: a) current/(extended to) time point, b) sequenced/time
range, c) non-sequenced/agnostic of time. The non-temporal baseline query B3
is a standard self-join: What (other) parts are supplied by the suppliers who
supplies part 55? Table 2 describes the semantics of each query.

Table 2. Bitemporal Dimension Queries

Name	App Time	System Time	System Time value
B3.1	Point	Point	Current
B3.2	Point	Point	Past
B3.3	Correlation	Point	Current
B3.4	Point	Correlation	-
B3.5	Correlation	Correlation	-
B3.6	Agnostic	Point	Current
B3.7	Agnostic	Point	Past
B3.8	Agnostic	Correlation	-
B3.9	Point	Agnostic	-
B3.10	Correlation	Agnostic	-
B3.11	Agnostic	Agnostic	-

5   Experiments

In order to validate the quality and usefulness of our benchmark, we carried out
a number of preliminary performance experiments on systems supporting temporal data. In addition, we added baselines for systems without native temporal
support by simulating temporal queries by means of additional columns which
represent the time dimension. More specifically, we execute the experiments on
System A, a relational DBMS supporting the temporal features of SQL:2011 as
well as on System B, an in-memory column store with basic system time support.
Since neither of these systems provides documentation on how to tune temporal
tables, we utilize out-of-the-box settings. All experiments were carried out on a
server with 192GB of DDR3-1066MHz RAM and 2 Intel Xeon X5675 processors
with 6 cores at 3.06 GHz running a Linux operating system. The execution was
staged and controlled using the Database Benchmarking Service [6].

   Most of our experiments were performed on data sizes with an initial data
scaling factor h of 1.0 and a history size m of 1.0. The most significant obstacle

that currently prohibits us from reaching larger scale factors is the loading process into the database servers. In order provide a suitable system time history for our measurements, individual update cases need to be performed as individual update transactions. The loading process is therefore rather time-consuming, as it cannot benefit from bulk loading. With this loading approach, the timestamps of the system time history are compressed to the period of the loading time, thus requiring adaptations when correlating system and application times.

5.1 Pure Timeslice

Our first measurement concerns the pure-timeslice queries introduced in Section 4.3. For each query we measure a uniform distribution of timestamps over each temporal dimension while keeping the other dimension to the current time, when needed. Figure 2 shows the results for both systems. System A sees relatively little variance since almost all queries have similar cost as full-history retrieval. The only notable exceptions are T3 and T4, which seem to pay an additional cost for the second time travel. System B shows more varied results: Establishing two system times in the same query is not possible, and generally the cost of system time operations exceeds that of application time. Yet, in all cases, more restricted queries yield better response times. Somewhat surprising is the high cost of implicit time travel to the current version (T7).

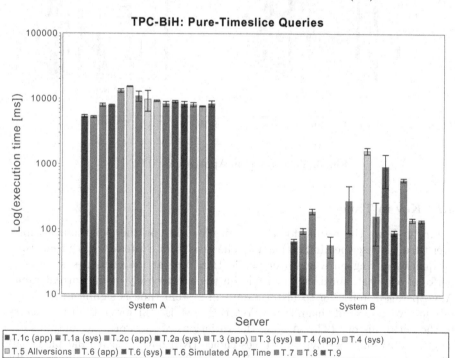

Fig. 2. Time Travel Operations

In order to understand the impact of time travel on complex application queries, we compare the TPC-H benchmark queries on the latest version stored in a normal table with time travel on these queries over temporal tables. As we can see in Figure 3, the impact strongly depends on the individual queries. While the majority of queries only see a small effect, other queries suffer from an order-of-magnitude slowdown (H17, H20). The exact causes need further study, one potential factor being range comparisons with sub queries.

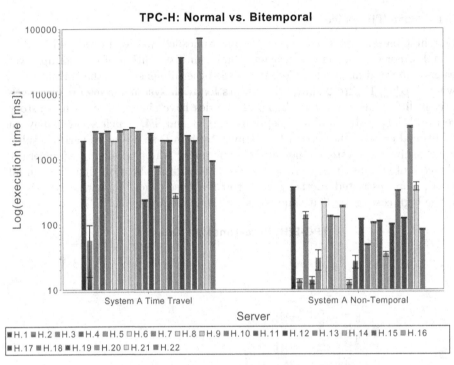

Fig. 3. Time Travel in Applications: TPC-H

5.2   Key in Time

Figure 4 shows the results for the queries focusing on the evolution of tuples over time, as described in Section 4.3. The results for System A show that using all queries relying on a key over application time at the current system time perform very fast, since they can rely on the primary key of the current table. Any operation referring to historic data in system time is significantly slower (about two orders of magnitude). Yet this cost is still lower than the access to the entire history (T5). Among the variations of the workload, only history length (K1a) and selectivity of tuples choice (K6) have a clear (and plausible) effect. The reduction of the temporal range (K2), projection of attributes (K3), version count ranges (K4) and previous versions (K5) end up costing the same – regardless if the time dimension is application time or system time. System B

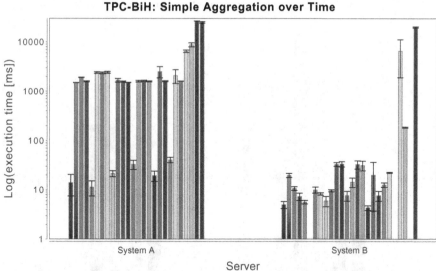

Fig. 4. Key in Time

also shows a performance gap between operations current system time and all other data, but it is much less pronounced. Similar effects exist for the value predicate selection.

5.3 Range-Timeslice

For the application-oriented queries in range-timeslice, we notice that the cost can become very significant (see Figure 5). To prevent very long experiment execution times, we measured this experiment on a smaller data set, containing data for h=0.1 and m=0.1. Nonetheless, we see that the more complex queries (R3 and R4) lead to serious problems: For System A, the response times of R3a and R3b (temporal aggregation) are more than two orders of magnitude more expensive than a full access to the history (measured in T5). While System B fares somewhat better on the T3 queries, it runs into a timeout after 1000 seconds on R4. Generally speaking, the higher raw performance of System B does not translate into lower response times for the remaining queries.

5.4 Bitemporal Dimensions

The results for combining all temporal dimensions with different types of operations (Figure 6) show some similar patterns: Measurements running purely on current system time perform rather well (3.1, 3.3, 3.5), whereas history accesses

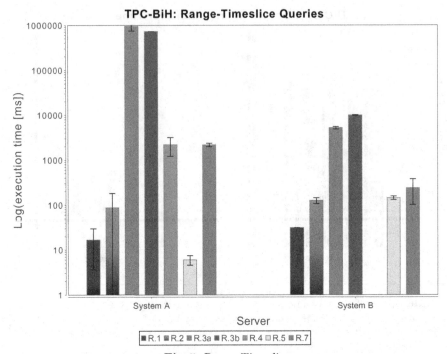

Fig. 5. Range-Timeslice

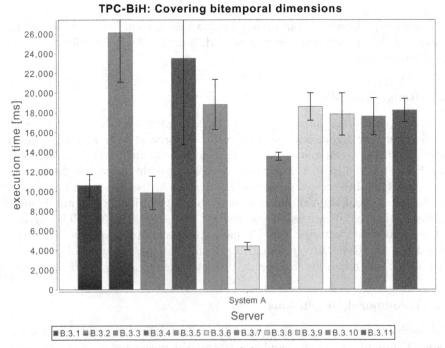

Fig. 6. Bitemporal dimensions

are expensive. Application time operations are cheapest when time can be ignored (3.5/3.6 vs 3.1/3.2), followed by temporal joins which are more expensive.

6   Conclusion

In this paper, we presented a benchmark for bitemporal databases which builds on existing benchmarks and presents a comprehensive coverage of temporal data and queries. Preliminary results on existing temporal database systems highlight significant optimization potential and insufficient support for common application use cases in the current SQL:2011 standard. We currently consider the following directions for future work: First, we want to broaden our evaluation, including larger data sets, DBMSs which we have not covered so far and possible tuning guidelines. This will give us further insights into which queries to add and possibly remove for a complete, yet concise coverage of the temporal DBMS workloads. Furthermore, we would like to incorporate explicit update queries, which we can evaluate in their performance characteristics.

References

1. Al-Kateb, M., Crolotte, A., Ghazal, A., Rose, L.: Adding a Temporal Dimension to the TPC-H Benchmark. In: Nambiar, R., Poess, M. (eds.) TPCTC 2012. LNCS, vol. 7755, pp. 51–59. Springer, Heidelberg (2013)
2. Cole, R., et al.: The Mixed Workload CH-benCHmark. In: DBTest, p. 8 (2011)
3. Gray, J.: Benchmark Handbook: For Database and Transaction Processing Systems. Morgan Kaufmann Publishers Inc., San Francisco (1992)
4. Jensen, C.S., et al.: A consensus test suite of temporal database queries. Tech. rep., Department of Computer Science, Aarhus University (1993)
5. Kalua, P.P., Robertson, E.L.: Benchmarking Temporal Databases - A Research Agenda. Tech. rep., Indiana University, Computer Science Department (1995)
6. Kaufmann, M., Fischer, P.M., Kossmann, D., May, N.: A Generic Database Benchmarking Service. In: ICDE (2013)
7. Kaufmann, M., Kossmann, D., May, N., Tonder, A.: Benchmarking Databases with History Support. Tech. report. ETH Zurich and SAP AG (2013)
8. Kaufmann, M., Manjili, A., Vagenas, P., Fischer, P., Kossmann, D., Faerber, F., May, N.: Timeline index: A unified data structure for processing queries on temporal data in SAP HANA. In: SIGMOD (2013)
9. Kulkarni, K.G., Michels, J.E.: Temporal Features in SQL: 2011. SIGMOD Record 41(3) (2012)
10. Salzberg, B., Tsotras, V.J.: Comparison of access methods for time-evolving data. ACM Comput. Surv. 31(2), 158–221 (1999)
11. Snodgrass, R.T.: Developing Time-Oriented Database Applications in SQL. Morgan Kaufmann (1999)
12. Snodgrass, R.T., et al.: TSQL2 language specification. SIGMOD Record 23(1) (1994)
13. Werstein, P.: A Performance Benchmark for Spatiotemporal Databases. In: Proc. of the 10th Annual Colloquium of the Spatial Information Research Centre, pp. 365–373 (1998)

Towards Comprehensive Measurement of Consistency Guarantees for Cloud-Hosted Data Storage Services

David Bermbach[1], Liang Zhao[2], and Sherif Sakr[2]

[1] Karlsruhe Institute of Technology
Karlsruhe, Germany
david.bermbach@kit.edu
[2] NICTA and University of New South Wales
Sydney, Australia
firstname.lastname@nicta.com.au

Abstract. The CAP theorem and the PACELC model have described the existence of direct trade-offs between consistency and availability as well as consistency and latency in distributed systems. Cloud storage services and NoSQL systems, both optimized for the web with high availability and low latency requirements, hence, typically opt to relax consistency guarantees. In particular, these systems usually offer eventual consistency which guarantees that all replicas will, in the absence of failures and further updates, eventually converge towards a consistent state where all replicas are identical. This, obviously, is a very imprecise description of actual guarantees.

Motivated by the popularity of eventually consistent storage systems, we take the position that a standard consistency benchmark is of great practical value. This paper is intended as a call for action; its goal is to motivate further research on building a standard comprehensive benchmark for quantifying the consistency guarantees of eventually consistent storage systems. We discuss the main challenges and requirements of such a benchmark, and present first steps towards a comprehensive consistency benchmark for cloud-hosted data storage systems. We evaluate our approach using experiments on both Cassandra and MongoDB.

1 Introduction

Recently, we have been witnessing an increasing adoption of cloud computing technologies in the IT industry. This new trend has created new needs for designing cloud-specific benchmarks that provide the ability to conduct comprehensive and powerful assessments for the performance characteristics of cloud-based systems and technologies [8, 15]. These benchmarks need to play an effective role in empowering cloud users to make better decisions regarding the selection of adequate systems and technologies that suit their application's requirements. In general, designing a good benchmark is a challenging task due to the many aspects that should be considered and which can influence the adoption and the

R. Nambiar and M. Poess (Eds.): TPCTC 2013, LNCS 8391, pp. 32–47, 2014.

usage scenarios of the benchmark. In particular, a benchmark is considered to be good if it can provide true and meaningful results for all of its stakeholders [17].

Over the past decade, rapidly growing Internet-based services such as e-mail, blogging, social networking, search and e-commerce have substantially redefined the way consumers communicate, access contents, share information and purchase products. Relational database management systems (RDBMS) have been considered as the *one-size-fits-all* solution for data persistence and retrieval for decades. However, the ever increasing need for scalability and new application requirements have created new challenges for traditional RDBMS. Recently, a new generation of low-cost, high-performance database systems, aptly named as NoSQL (Not Only SQL), has emerged to challenge the dominance of RDBMS. The main features of these systems include: ability to scale horizontally while guaranteeing low latency and high availability, flexible schemas and data models, and simple low-level query interfaces instead of rich query languages [22].

In general, the CAP theorem [10] and the PACELC model [1] describe the existence of direct tradeoffs between consistency and availability as well as consistency and latency. These trade-offs are a continuum, so that, due to the popularity of NoSQL systems, there is now a plethora of storage systems covering a broad range of consistency guaranteess. In practice, most cloud storage services and NoSQL systems (e.g., Amazon SimpleDB[1], Amazon Dynamo [14], Google BigTable [11], Cassandra [19], HBase[2]) opt for low latency and high availability and, hence, apply a relaxed consistency policy called *eventual consistency* [25] which guarantees that all replicas will, in the absence of failures and further updates, eventually converge towards a consistent state where all replicas are identical. For situations without failures, the maximum size of the inconsistency window can be bounded based on factors such as communication delays, the load on the system, and the number of replicas involved in the replication scheme, e.g., see [3]. In practice, the implementation and the performance of the eventually consistent mechanism could vary between systems depending on several factors such as the data replication and synchronization protocols, the system load etc. For example, the results of [5] cannot be entirely explained by the aforementioned influence factors.

Motivated by the increasing popularity of eventually consistent cloud-hosted data storage systems, we take the position that a standard consistency measurement benchmark for cloud-hosted data storage system is of great practical value. For example, in cloud environments, users often want to monitor the performance of their services in order to ensure that they meet their Service Level Agreements (SLAs). Therefore, if consistency guarantees are specified as part of the SLA of a cloud-hosted data storage service and the severity of SLA violations can be detected and quantified in an agreeable way, then users could at least receive some monetary compensation.

Furthermore, we believe that a comprehensive consistency benchmark is necessary to evaluate the emerging flow of eventually consistent storage systems.

---

[1] http://aws.amazon.com/simpledb/

[2] http://hbase.apache.org/

Such a consistency benchmark should be able to provide a clear picture of the relationship between the performance of the system under consideration, the benchmarking workloads, the pattern of failures and the different consistency metrics that can be measured from both of the system perspective and the client perspective. This paper is intended as a call for action; its goal is to motivate further research on building a standard benchmark for quantifying consistency guarantees and behavior of cloud-hosted data storage systems. In this paper, we do not present a comprehensive benchmark that would address all the challenges such a benchmark would need to consider. We do, however, define the main requirements for designing and building this benchmark and present the first steps towards a comprehensive consistency benchmark. In particular, we summarize the main contributions of this paper as follows:

- The identification of the challenges that a comprehensive consistency benchmark should consider.
- An analysis of state-of-the-art consistency benchmarking of NoSQL systems.
- The extension of an existing benchmarking approach towards meeting the defined consistency measurement challenges.
- An experimental evaluation of two popular NoSQL systems, Cassandra [19] and MongoDB[3].

The reminder of this paper is organized as follows. We start with some background on consistency perspectives as well as consistency metrics and identify challenges of a comprehensive consistency benchmark in section 2. Next, in section 3 we describe the extensible architecture of a consistency benchmarking system and its implementation. Afterwards, we use our proposed system for evaluating and analyzing the effects of geo-replication under different workloads on the performance of consistency guarantees for Cassandra and MongoDB in section 4. Section 5 summarizes the related work before we conclude the paper in Section 6.

2   Consistency Measurement: Perspectives, Metrics and Challenges

2.1   Consistency Perspectives

There are two main perspectives on consistency measurement: the perspective of the *provider* of a storage system and the perspective of a *client* of such a system. The provider perspective focuses on the internal synchronization processes and the communication between replicas and is, hence, called *data-centric* consistency. In contrast, the client perspective focuses on the consistency guarantees that a client will be able to observe. This perspective is called *client-centric* consistency [24]. Depending on the perspective, different aspects need to be measured. Figure 1 shows a schematic overview of both consistency perspectives.

---

[3] `mongodb.org`

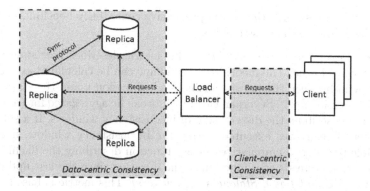

Fig. 1. Data-centric and Client-centric Consistency Perspectives

For both perspectives, there are two dimensions: *staleness* and *ordering*. Staleness describes how much a replica (or a datum returned to the client) lags behind in comparison to the newest version. It can be expressed both in terms of time or versions and most real world applications can tolerate small staleness values. Data-centric staleness is an upper bound for client-centric staleness [5].

Ordering on the other hand is more critical. It describes how updates are executed on replicas for data-centric consistency and what kind of operation ordering becomes visible to clients for client-centric consistency models. Typical data-centric models like *Sequential Consistency* or *Causal Consistency* [24] do not consider staleness and can be ordered by their strictness. Typical client-centric ordering models like monotonic reads or read your writes are disjunct in their guarantees [6, 24].

2.2 Metrics

From the data-centric consistency perspective, consistency metrics (e.g., staleness or violations of certain ordering models) can be easily determined by analyzing detailed logs created by the different replicas. It is therefore not possible to quantify data-centric consistency for hosted cloud storage services (e.g., Amazon S3) as access to the machines running the actual replicas is required. On the other hand, analyzing those logs after running a standard database benchmark is relatively straightforward. Based on previous work [3, 5, 6], we propose to use fine-grained client-centric metrics. These are useful to an application developer as they provide direct insight into the guarantees an application will encounter and can be measured with any kind of storage system which is treated as a black box. This is also a common practice for measuring the performance benchmarks of database[4] and NoSQL systems [12, 20]. Furthermore, using such an approach does not preclude the usage of replica logs (if available) to also determine data-centric consistency guarantees.

---

[4] tpc.org

In principle, we suggest that a comprehensive consistency benchmark should include the following staleness metrics:

- *Time-Based Staleness (t-visibility)*: This metric describes how stale a read is in terms of time. The inconsistency window can be calculated as the time window in between the latest possible read of version n and the start of the write of version $n+1$. Several measurements can be aggregated into a density function describing the distribution of inconsistency windows. If a sufficient number of reads was executed during the inconsistency window, it is also possible to report a cumulative density function describing the likelihood of fresh and stale reads as a function of the duration since the last update.
- *Operation Count-Based Staleness (k-staleness)*: This metric is based on the number of intervening writes and measures the degree of staleness. It obviously depends on the write load on the system and can, thus, be expressed as a function of the write load combined with t-visibility.

Regarding the ordering dimension, the following four client-centric consistency models have been proposed, e.g., see [24, 25]:

- *Monotonic Read Consistency (MRC)*: After reading a version n, a client will never again read an older version.
- *Monotonic Write Consistency (MWC)*: Two writes by the same client will (eventually but always) be serialized in chronological order.
- *Read Your Writes Consistency (RYWC)*: After writing a version n, the same client will never again read an older version.
- *Write Follows Read Consistency (WFRC)*: After reading a version n, an update by the same client will only execute on replicas that are at least as new as version n.

For these four models, we propose to use the likelihood of a violation as metrics. WFRC is usually not directly visible to a client and is therefore hard to determine without access to the replica servers' logs. A standard benchmark, hence, need only include measurements of MRC, RYWC and MWC.

2.3   Measurement Challenges

Accuracy and Meaningfulness of Measurements. In general, fine-grained metrics are better for controlling the quality of a system than coarse-grained metrics as they allow the definition of more expressive tradeoff decisions between conflicting design decisions. In practice, an accurate measurement for consistency metrics is a challenging process. For example, the accuracy of client-centric t-visibility measurements is directly influenced by the precision of the clock synchronization protocol. There are several synchronization protocols that work for different scenarios. For example, NTP[5] which is frequently used in distributed systems offers about single digit millisecond accuracy

In addition, apart from workloads which may run in parallel to the benchmark and, thus, use different system resources up to saturation levels, there is also the

---

[5] ntp.org

workload (or rather the interaction pattern between benchmarking clients and datastore) of the benchmark itself. Our experience has shown that observed consistency ordering guarantees are highly volatile in regards to small changes in this workload pattern (e.g., see [7]). Also, there is much interdependency between the actual storage system, the load balancer used and the application implementation. All in all, this leads to a situation where it is very hard to precisely reproduce a concrete workload on one storage system, not to mention on more than one, in a comparable way.

In large numbers of experiments, we have seen that more simplistic workloads are easier to reproduce and, thus, allow a fairer comparison of systems. At the same time, such a workload is not necessarily representative of an actual application. Storage systems with at least causally consistent guarantees will assert those guarantees independent of the actual workload. For eventually consistent systems, though, some systems might (depending on the load balancer strategy as well as the actual workload) behave like a strictly consistent database in one scenario and become completely inconsistent in another. To us, the best strategy for measuring the ordering dimension is still an unsolved challenge. We believe, though, that reproducible and comparable results are paramount to benchmarking whereas application-specific measurements belong in the area of consistency monitoring. Hence, we tend to favor more simplistic workloads.

Staleness, on the other hand, can be measured independent of benchmarking workloads. Finally, measurement results should be meaningful to application developers in that measured values have a direct impact on application design.

Workloads. Modern web-based application are often periodically demanding (e.g. on specific day, month or time of the year) or create bursty workloads that may grow very rapidly before shrinking back to previous normal levels [9]. Ideally, a cloud-hosted data storage service should be infinitely scalable and instantaneously elastic and, thus, be able to handle such a load variance. In particular, a perfectly elastic cloud-hosted storage system should scale up or out its resources indefinitely with increasing workload, and this should happen instantly as the workload increases with no degradation on the application performance.

However, reality is not perfect: In practice, systems use different mechanisms to scale horizontally. For example, when new nodes are added to the cluster, Cassandra moves data stored on the old nodes to the new nodes that have just been bootstrapped. HBase, in contrast, acts as a cache for the data stored in the underlying distributed file system and pulls data only on cache misses. Clearly, reducing the amount of the data that needs to be moved during the bootstrapping process asserts that the system will reach its stable state faster with less congestion on system resources. In other scenarios, live migration techniques are used in a multi-tenancy environment to migrate the tenant with excessive workload to less loaded server in order to cope with increasing workload.

These different implementations for the different systems could affect the consistency guarantees in different ways during the scaling process and should, hence, be considered within a comprehensive assessment of a storage system's consistency guarantees. Previous studies did not consider different workloads (e.g., sinusoidal workloads, exponentially bursty workloads, linearly increasing workload, random workload) and how the system's process of coping with it affects consistency guarantees.

Geo-replication. In general, Cloud computing is a model for building scalable and highly available low latency services on top of an elastic pool of configurable virtualized resources such as virtual machines, storage services and virtualized networks. These resources can be located in multiple data centers that are geographically located in different places around the world which provides the ability to build an affordable geo-scalable cloud-hosted data storage service that can cope with volatile workloads. In practice, most of the commercial cloud storage services such as Amazon S3 or SimpleDB do not use wide area replication (only within a region). However, other systems such as PNUTS [23], Megastore [4] and Spanner [13] have been specifically designed for geo-replicated deployments. Using compute services, it is easily possible to deploy geo-replicated NoSQL systems of any kind.

Zhao et al. [28,29] have conducted an experimental evaluation of the performance characteristics of asynchronous database replication of database servers which are hosted in virtual machines using wide area replication. The results of the study show that an increased application workload directly affects the update propagation time. However, as the number of database replicas increases, the replication delay decreases. Obviously, the replication delay is more affected by the workload increase than the configurations of the geographic location of the database replicas. So far, there is no study that has considered measuring the consistency guarantees of cloud-hosted data storage services in geo-replicated deployments. This issue should be considered in a comprehensive consistency benchmark. Specifically, such a benchmark should analyze the impact of different levels of geo-distribution on consistency guarantees.

Multi-tenancy. Multi-tenancy is an optimization mechanism for cloud-hosted services in which multiple customers are consolidated onto the same system so that the economy of scale principles help to effectively drive down the operational cost. One challenge of multi-tenancy in cloud storage services is to achieve complete resource separation and performance isolation of tenants hosted on the same physical server. In practice, the performance for any hosted tenant can turn to be a function of the workloads of other tenants hosted on the same server. A comprehensive benchmark should consider all kinds of cross-effects that could happen between the different tenants.

Node Failure Consideration. Inconsistencies in cloud storage systems are often caused by failures. While it is certainly interesting to consider failures, this is not possible when running black box tests, e.g., against cloud storage services, where injecting artificial failures is not an option. If access to the replica servers is possible, a comprehensive benchmark should also consider the effects of different failure types (e.g., node crash-stop, crash-recover or byzantine) on the consistency guarantees of the underlying storage system.

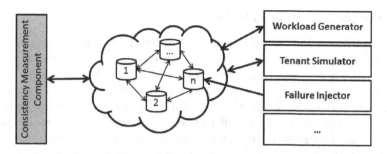

Fig. 2. Benchmark Architecture

3 Consistency Benchmark Design

3.1 Benchmark Architecture

A comprehensive consistency benchmark needs to consider the challenges pointed out in the previous section. From a more technical perspective, it is desirable to reuse existing components and to assert that the benchmark is extensible and flexible. We propose to use a plugin model where the component which is actually measuring consistency is augmented with additional modules if desired. Figure 2 illustrates the basic architecture of our framework with the following main components:

- **Workload Generator:** This component is used to create different work-loads on the system to allow the quantification of consistency effects during phases of resource saturation. It should also report results for standard performance metrics like latency or throughput to quantify tradeoffs between consistency and performance.
- **Tenant Simulator:** The Tenant Simulator is used to create a specific kind of behavior for individually simulated tenants of a storage system. While the workload generator just creates load on the system, this component might create a more detailed behavior of a single tenant so that multi-tenant cross-effects on consistency can be studied.
- **Consistency Measurement Component (CMC):** This is the component which is responsible for measuring the consistency guarantees of the underlying system. Its output should use meaningful and fine-grained consistency metrics from a client perspective.
- **Failure Injector:** The Failure Injector is a component which can be used with self-hosted storage systems and can cause a variety of failures.

It could also be reasonable to include a benchmark scheduling and deployment component, e.g., [18], to ease benchmarking of various configurations and systems.

3.2   Benchmark Implementation

For the implementation, we propose to reuse existing, proven tools and to patch them together using shell scripts. The consistency benchmarking tool of Bermbach and Tai [5] has been used for a large number of consistency benchmarks with various storage systems and services. We extended it slightly to also measure violations of RYWC and MWC so that it, combined with the existing code, measures data for all metrics discussed above. As these continuous, and thus fine-grained, consistency metrics take a client perspective they should be meaningful to application developers. As the benchmarking approach itself relies on a distributed deployment it lends itself to studying the effects of geo-replication. An extension, measuring consistency after delete operations, is currently being developed. Therefore, we will use this tool as our CMC.

The Yahoo! Cloud Servicing Benchmark (YCSB) [12] is the most well known benchmarking framework for NoSQL databases. The tool supports different NoSQL databases and various kinds of workloads and has been designed to be extensible in both dimensions. We will use it as our Workload Generator Component.

So far, we have not included implementations for a Tenant Simulator which is ongoing work at KIT. We have also not used a Failure Injector but Simian Army[6], which was published as open source by Netflix[7], is a promising candidate for future experiments.

The benchmarking tool is extensible for use with all kinds of storage systems. Both our CMC as well as YCSB use an adapter model where the tool itself interacts only with an abstract interface while concrete implementations describe the mapping to the storage system itself. The CMC requires only a key-value interface (even though more complex interfaces can be studied as well) which can be fulfilled by all kinds of systems. YCSB uses the abstract operations insert, update, delete, read and scan for different workloads. Depending on the system itself and the kind of workloads whose influence shall be studied, different combinations of those operations can be used. A Failure Injector could also use a multi-cloud library to create machine failures as well as a similar database adapter framework to cause database failures. The Tenant Simulator could use the same adapter framework as YCSB.

4   Evaluation

To show the applicability of our consistency benchmarking approach, we studied how geo-distribution of replicas combined with two different workloads affects the consistency guarantees of Cassandra and MongoDB. We chose these systems as Cassandra is a popular example of a peer-to-peer system whereas MongoDB is typically (and was during our tests) configured in a master slave setup.

---

[6] github.com/Netflix/SimianArmy
[7] netflix.com

4.1 Experiment Setup

For our evaluation, we ran the following three benchmarks on Amazon EC2[8], each with Cassandra and MongoDB:

- **Single-AZ:** All replicas were deployed in the region *eu-west* within the same availability zone[9].
- **Multi-AZ:** One replica is deployed in each of the three availability zones of the region *eu-west*.
- **Multi-Region:** One replica is deployed in three different regions: *eu-west*, *us-west* (northern California) and *asia-pacific* (Singapore).

All replicas were deployed on *m1.medium* instances, whereas the CMC was running on *m1.small* instances distributed according to the respective test. YCSB was deployed on an *m1.xlarge* instance. Both YCSB and the writer machine of the Consistency Measurement Component as well as the MongoDB master were deployed in the *eu-west-1a* availability zone. We used a simple load balancer strategy for all tests, where requests were always routed to the closest replica. Cassandra clients were configured to use consistency level ONE for all requests.

During each test, we left the storage system at idle for at least 30 minutes before we started the Consistency Measurement Component. After another 30 minutes we then started YCSB running workload 1. When YCSB was done, we again waited for the storage system to stabilize before running workload 2. Finally, after completing workload 2, we asserted that the system stabilized again at the levels before each workload. This resulted in about 1000 to 1300 writes of the CMC per benchmark for which we measured our consistency metrics.

There were no cross effects between the three different tests as we started each storage system cluster from scratch. Both workloads comprised one million operations on 1000 records. Workload 1 had 80% reads and 20% writes, while workload 2 was configured the other way around.

4.2 Results

Effects of Workload. Surprisingly, the workloads barely affected the inconsistency window (t-visibility) of both systems. We used Amazon CloudWatch to also measure the CPU utilization and network IO of the replicas and the YCSB instance. In all cases network IO of the "master" replica[10] seemed to be the bottleneck. During one benchmark, while we were still testing the setup of our scripts, we managed to overload the CPU of Cassandra's "master" replica. During that period we observed very high staleness values. Obviously, when the CPU is saturated, the consistency behavior becomes completely unpredictable. Table 1 shows the CPU utilization that we encountered during our experiments.

---

[8] `aws.amazon.com/ec2`

[9] On AWS, availability zones describe completely independent data centers located next to each other within the same geographical region. AWS regions each have at least two availability zones and are geographically distributed.

[10] The load balancing strategy that we chose effectively asserted that all updates originated on the same replica.

Table 1. CPU Utilization During Consistency Benchmarks

		Workload			
System	Replica Type	idle	CMC only	read-heavy	update-heavy
Cassandra	Update Coordinator	<5%	ca. 20%	70-80%	70-80%
	Other Replica	<5%	15-20%	ca. 25%	25-40%
MongoDB	Master	<5%	20%	ca. 25%	35-40%
	Slave	<5%	5-10%	ca. 25%	35-40%

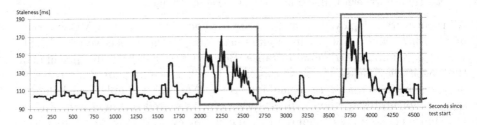

Fig. 3. Change of Staleness over Time (Cassandra, Multi-region Setup)

During one of the tests (Cassandra in the multi-region setup), we were able to see an effect of the workloads on the inconsistency window. Figure 3 shows how staleness values changed over time during that experiment (the graph shows a moving average to remove extreme values). The boxes indicate the periods during which the two workloads were running.

4.3 Effects of Geo-distribution

For Cassandra, about 98% of all requests created an inconsistency window between zero and one milliseconds when deployed within a single availability zone. As there was only a single maximum value of 38ms, we do not show a chart for this. For the setups where replicas were distributed over three availability zones or regions respectively, Figure 4 shows the observed density functions for the inconsistency windows. We have excluded extreme values from our results to increase clarity of the chart. As expected, it is fairly obvious that increasing the level of geo-distribution increases staleness. We did not encounter any violations of MRC, MWC or RYWC which is caused by both the load balancing strategy that we chose (routing requests to the closest replica) as well as the fact that our benchmarks did not encounter any obvious failures.

For MongoDB, the results were slightly different. As expected, the setup with replicas distributed over different regions showed the longest inconsistency window. We would have expected to see again a value of close to zero for the single availability zone setup and a slightly larger value for the setup in multiple availability zones. Interestingly though, this was exactly the other way around. See Figure 5 for the density functions of observed inconsistency windows on MongoDB.

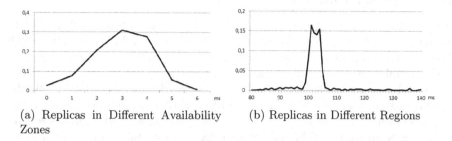

(a) Replicas in Different Availability Zones

(b) Replicas in Different Regions

Fig. 4. Distribution of Inconsistency Windows in Cassandra

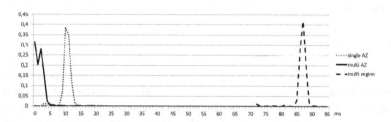

Fig. 5. Distribution of Inconsistency Windows in MongoDB

When looking at the detailed results for the individual replicas[11], it becomes obvious that it was always the same replica that was lagging behind. When we excluded this replica, results are again as expected: More than 96% of all requests show an inconsistency window of 5ms or less in the single availability zone setup. We believe that this could be caused by one of two effects which are both related to problems with the respective virtual machine. Either the third replica had a problem (possibly due to a resource-greedy tenant on the same physical machine) and was really lagging behind or the CMC reader for this replica had a clock synchronization issue which caused its clock to lag by around 10ms behind. Normally, this should not be an issue as our CMC component was started about 24 hours in advance to allow for a slow clock synchronization process[12]. In this case, one possible reason for causing this effect is a problem with the virtual machine of the CMC reader. However, further investigation is required to verify if other reasons could be behind this effect.

During our multi-region tests with both Cassandra and MongoDB, we could observe that the Singapore region usually added another 15 to 20ms to the inconsistency window already caused by the *us-west* replica. Obviously, the connection to the Singapore replica was the limiting factor in our setup.

---

[11] We do not report those detailed results here due to space limitations, but the CMC logs the result of every single datastore interaction as well as the corresponding timestamp and latency.

[12] `ntp.org` recommends about 4 hours, so we really played it safe here.

4.4 Additional Observations

For Cassandra, we also repeated a multi-region setup with a fourth replica in the region *sao-paulo* and varied the write consistency level of Cassandra which describes the number of replicas that need to acknowledge a write request so that it terminates successfully. In all of our tests, we could not see any variance in the staleness levels due to the write consistency level chosen. Obviously, the write consistency level is rather a durability level than a consistency level as the system does not block dirty reads. This implies that in a geo-distributed setting the updates might be visible on some replicas before the request commits at the coordinator of the write which, in essence, corresponds to something like "negative staleness". Apart from increased request latency there was no effect on the system.

5 Related Work

Several studies have been presented as an attempt to quantify the consistency guarantees of cloud storage services. Wada et al. [26] presented an approach for measuring time-based staleness by writing timestamps to a key from one client, reading the same key and computing the difference between the reader's local time and the timestamp read. However, this approach is very primitive and imprecise and is, hence, unsuitable in a production environment. In particular, systems often use a certain degree of sessions stickiness so that most inconsistencies will never become visible to the single client. Arguably, a more complex interaction pattern between benchmarking client and datastore could also be interesting. These limitations hurt the accuracy and meaningfulness of the reported measurements. Bermbach and Tai [5] have addressed parts of these limitations by extending the original experiments of [26] using a number of readers which are geographically distributed. They measure the inconsistency window by calculating the difference between the latest read timestamp of version n and the write timestamp of version $n + 1$. Their experiments with Amazon S3 showed that the system frequently violates monotonic read consistency and exposes very high degrees of staleness. Using the individual reader's read timestamps their approach also allows to easily describe monotonic reads violations as well as the probability of reading fresh or stale data (including the degree of staleness) as a function of the duration since the last update. The accuracy of their measurements in contrast to the single reader-writer setup, though, is limited by the accuracy of the clock synchronization protocol used.

Anderson et al. [2] and Golab et al. [16] presented an offline algorithm and its online analysis extension that builds a dependency graph based on the clients' operation logs and searches for cycles in that graph. Their approach allows to check for violations of safety, regularity and atomicity which are properties developed by the theoretical distributed systems community. It is unclear what the implications of their results are for both system providers (data-centric view) or application developers (client-centric view). Rahman et al. [21] have presented a first step towards defining a standard consistency measurement benchmark and extended their previous work to also consider, e.g., Δ-atomicity and k-atomicity. k-atomicity describes an atomic execution where a maximum version lag of k units could be observed. Δ-atomicity does the same for time. We believe that these metrics are insufficient for benchmarking consistency guarantees of cloud storage systems for several reasons: First, these metrics are very coarse-grained in that they just return the single maximum inconsistency value which could be observed. For example, in the results of [5] only the highest measurement spike would be reported. Second, although these metrics are from a client perspective, it is unclear how they might be helpful to an application developer. Third, the measurements are highly dependent on the client workload and are, thus, likely to be not reproducible. We believe that their approach is, hence, more suitable for monitoring a consistency health status for a production application where it may be necessary to react to severe consistency violations whereas for benchmarking purposes more detailed metrics are needed which provide meaningful information to application developers.

Zellag and Kemme [27] have proposed an approach for real-time detection of consistency anomalies for arbitrary cloud applications accessing various types of cloud datastores in transactional or non-transactional contexts. In particular, the approach builds the dependency graph during the execution of a cloud application and detect cycles in the graph at the application layer and independently of the underlying datastore. One of their main assumptions though, that of a causally consistent datastore, makes it impractical to use with today's eventually consistent storage systems. We expect future extensions to resolve this issue.

Bailis et al. [3] presented an approach that provides expected bounds on staleness by predicting the behavior of eventually consistent quorum-replicated data stores using Monte Carlo simulations and an abstract model of the storage system including details such as the distribution of latencies for network links. In general, predicting staleness, if accurate, can be used in a variety of ways, such as performance tuning, monitoring system service level agreements and feedback control. Still, a simulation approach is inherently limited in its accuracy as it is only an approximation based on the influence factors considered within the model. Furthermore, PBS is limited to Dynamo-style quorum systems and, thus, not applicable to systems like MongoDB.

Patil et al. [20] also propose to measure staleness in terms of time. Their benchmarking approach, though, can only serve as a rough approximation for consistency as it is subject to the same limitations as the approach described by Wada et al. [26] and also incurs additional inaccuracies due to the way values are measured.

6 Conclusion

In this paper, we presented the first steps for building a standard comprehensive benchmark for quantifying the consistency guarantees of cloud-hosted storage systems. We identified meaningful and fine-grained continuous metrics, the main challenges and requirements for such a benchmark and proposed an architecture for a corresponding benchmarking system. Afterwards, we showed how a comprehensive benchmarking tool could be built reusing proven, standard components. We then used this benchmarking tool to evaluate the effects of geo-replication and different workloads on two popular NoSQL systems, Cassandra and MongoDB, and also studied how different write quorums in Cassandra affect consistency.

In future work, we plan to also include a Tenant Simulator and a Failure Injector, as outlined in section 3, and use it to study the effects of various kinds of failures as well as cross-tenant effects on consistency guarantees of eventually consistent storage systems. We also plan to run additional benchmarks on other storage systems in all kinds of consistency benchmark setups using the components presented within this work. Furthermore, we intend to continue our efforts towards a standardized comprehensive consistency benchmark comparable to performance benchmarks like TPC-W.

References

1. Abadi, D.: Consistency tradeoffs in modern distributed database system design: Cap is only part of the story. Computer 45(2) (2012)
2. Anderson, E., Li, X., Shah, M.A., Tucek, J., Wylie, J.J.: What consistency does your key-value store actually provide? In: HotDep (2010)
3. Bailis, P., Venkataraman, S., Franklin, M., Hellerstein, J., Stoica, I.: Probabilistically bounded staleness for practical partial quorums. PVLDB 5(8) (2012)
4. Baker, J., Bond, C., Corbett, J., Furman, J., Khorlin, A., Larson, J., Léon, J.M., Li, Y., Lloyd, A., Yushprakh, V.: Megastore: Providing scalable, highly available storage for interactive services. In: Proc. of CIDR, pp. 223–234 (2011)
5. Bermbach, D., Tai, S.: Eventual consistency: How soon is eventual? an evaluation of amazon s3's consistency behavior. In: Proceedings of the 6th Workshop on Middleware for Service Oriented Computing (2011)
6. Bermbach, D., Kuhlenkamp, J.: Consistency in distributed storage systems: An overview of models, metrics and measurement approaches. In: Gramoli, V., Guerraoui, R. (eds.) NETYS 2013. LNCS, vol. 7853, pp. 175–189. Springer, Heidelberg (2013)
7. Bermbach, D., Kuhlenkamp, J., Derre, B., Klems, M., Tai, S.: A middleware guaranteeing client-centric consistency on top of eventually consistent datastores. In: Proceedings of the 1st International Conference on Cloud Engineering (IC2E). IEEE (2013)
8. Binnig, C., Kossmann, D., Kraska, T., Loesing, S.: How is the weather tomorrow?: towards a benchmark for the cloud. In: Proceedings of the Second International Workshop on Testing Database Systems (2009)
9. Bodík, P., Fox, A., Franklin, M.J., Jordan, M.I., Patterson, D.A.: Characterizing, modeling, and generating workload spikes for stateful services. In: SoCC (2010)
10. Brewer, E.A.: Towards robust distributed systems (abstract). In: PODC (2000)
11. Chang, F., Dean, J., Ghemawat, S., Hsieh, W.C., Wallach, D.A., Burrows, M., Chandra, T., Fikes, A., Gruber, R.E.: Bigtable: A Distributed Storage System for Structured Data. ACM Trans. Comput. Syst. 26(2) (2008)
12. Cooper, B.F., Silberstein, A., Tam, E., Ramakrishnan, R., Sears, R.: Benchmarking cloud serving systems with ycsb. In: Proceedings of the 1st ACM Symposium on Cloud Computing, pp. 143–154. ACM (2010)

13. Corbett, J.C., Dean, J., Epstein, M., Fikes, A., Frost, C., Furman, J., Ghemawat, S., Gubarev, A., Heiser, C., Hochschild, P., et al.: Spanner: Google's globally-distributed database. To appear in Proceedings of OSDI, p. 1 (2012)
14. DeCandia, G., Hastorun, D., Jampani, M., Kakulapati, G., Lakshman, A., Pilchin, A., Sivasubramanian, S., Vosshall, P., Vogels, W.: Dynamo: amazon's highly available key-value store. In: SOSP (2007)
15. Folkerts, E., Alexandrov, A., Sachs, K., Iosup, A., Markl, V., Tosun, C.: Benchmarking in the Cloud: What It Should, Can, and Cannot Be. In: Nambiar, R., Poess, M. (eds.) TPCTC 2012. LNCS, vol. 7755, pp. 173–188. Springer, Heidelberg (2013)
16. Golab, W., Li, X., Shah, M.: Analyzing consistency properties for fun and profit. In: Proceedings of the 30th Annual ACM SIGACT-SIGOPS Symposium on Principles of Distributed Computing, pp. 197–206. ACM (2011)
17. Gray, J. (ed.): The Benchmark Handbook for Database and Transaction Systems, 1st edn. Morgan Kaufmann (1991)
18. Klems, M., Bermbach, D., Weinert, R.: A runtime quality measurement framework for cloud database service systems. In: Proceedings of the 8th International Conference on the Quality of Information and Communications Technology. Springer (2012)
19. Lakshman, A., Malik, P.: Cassandra: A structured storage system on a p2p network. In: Proceedings of the Twenty-First Annual Symposium on Parallelism in Algorithms and Architectures, pp. 47–47. ACM (2009)
20. Patil, S., Polte, M., Ren, K., Tantisiriroj, W., Xiao, L., López, J., Gibson, G., Fuchs, A., Rinaldi, B.: Ycsb++: benchmarking and performance debugging advanced features in scalable table stores. In: Proceedings of the 2nd ACM Symposium on Cloud Computing, p. 9. ACM (2011)
21. Rahman, M.R., Golab, W.M., AuYoung, A., Keeton, K., Wylie, J.J.: Toward a Principled Framework for Benchmarking Consistency. In: HotDep (2012)
22. Sakr, S., Liu, A., Batista, D.M., Alomari, M.: A Survey of Large Scale Data Management Approaches in Cloud Environments. IEEE Communications Surveys and Tutorials 13(3), 311–336 (2011)
23. Silberstein, A., Chen, J., Lomax, D., McMillan, B., Mortazavi, M., Narayan, P.P.S., Ramakrishnan, R., Sears, R.: PNUTS in Flight: Web-Scale Data Serving at Yahoo. IEEE Internet Computing 16(1) (2012)
24. Tanenbaum, A.S., van Steen, M.: Distributed systems: principles and paradigms, 2nd edn. Pearson, Prentice Hall, Upper Saddle River, NJ (2007)
25. Vogels, W.: Eventually Consistent. Queue 6 (October 2008), http://doi.acm.org/10.1145/1466443.1466448
26. Wada, H., Fekete, A., Zhao, L., Lee, K., Liu, A.: Data Consistency Properties and the Trade-offs in Commercial Cloud Storage: the Consumers' Perspective. In: CIDR (2011)
27. Zellag, K., Kemme, B.: How Consistent is your Cloud Application? In: SoCC (2012)
28. Zhao, L., Sakr, S., Fekete, A., Wada, H., Liu, A.: Application-Managed Database Replication on Virtualized Cloud Environments. In: ICDE Workshops on Data Management in the Cloud (DMC) (2012)
29. Zhao, L., Sakr, S., Liu, A.: Application-Managed Replication Controller for Cloud-Hosted Databases. In: IEEE CLOUD (2012)

TPC Express – A New Path for TPC Benchmarks

Karl Huppler[1] and Douglas Johnson[2]

[1] Independent
karlhuppler@gmail.com
[2] InfoSizing
doug@sizing.com

Abstract. To accommodate differences in systems architecture and DBMS functions and features, the TPC has long held that the best way to define a database benchmark is to author a paper specification of the application to be measured, leaving the implementation of that specification to the individual analyst. While this technique allows for the optimal implementation for a specific DBMS on a specific platform, it makes the initial entry into benchmark development a costly one – often cost prohibitive. The TPC has embarked on a plan to develop a new benchmark category, dubbed TPC Express, where benchmarks based on predefined, executable kits that can be rapidly deployed and measured. This paper defines the TPC Express model, contrasts it to the TPC's existing "Enterprise" model, and highlights many of the changes needed within the TPC to ensure the Express model is a successful one.

Keywords: Performance, Benchmark, Database, Servers.

1 Introduction

To accommodate differences in systems architecture and DBMS functions and features, the Transaction Processing Performance Council (TPC) has long held that the best way to define a database benchmark is to author a paper specification of the application to be measured, leaving the implementation of that specification to the individual analyst. While this technique allows for the optimal implementation for a specific DBMS on a specific platform, it makes the initial entry into benchmark development a costly one – often cost prohibitive.

Although members of the TPC have looked for solutions to this challenge for several years, the work discussed in this paper was initiated in early 2012, by one of the TPC's affiliates, InfoSizing. The TPC contracted with InfoSizing to deliver a summary overview of steps and processes needed to shift to a benchmark format that retained the current strengths of the TPC, while removing or diminishing current impediments in the existing TPC benchmark model.

As a result of this work and research from the leadership in the TPC, the TPC has embarked on a plan to develop a new benchmark category, dubbed TPC Express,

R. Nambiar and M. Poess (Eds.): TPCTC 2013, LNCS 8391, pp. 48–60, 2014.
© Springer International Publishing Switzerland 2014

where benchmarks are based on predefined, executable kits that can be rapidly deployed and measured. This paper defines the TPC Express model, contrasts it to the TPC's existing "Enterprise" model, and highlights the many changes needed within the TPC to ensure the Express model is a successful one.

Caveat: This paper is based on a "work in progress." As the work progresses, it is likely that improvements will be made and some decisions will go in a direction that is different than is indicated, here. This paper is not a guarantee of the outcome, but rather an indicator of what is certain to be an exciting development within the TPC.

2   Pros and Cons of the TPC's Current Benchmark Model

There is little question that the TPC's existing model for enterprise database benchmarks was a good one when the TPC first started developing benchmarks in 1989 and the early 1990s. Database products delivered solutions in very different ways and most enterprise customers had private development teams that would create custom applications for the enterprise, using the hardware, operating system and DBMS of choice.

The TPC's choice to deliver, instead of explicit executable code, a functional specification for a benchmark application was novel. It allowed benchmark teams to develop and deliver the best possible application for their environment. This "Enterprise" benchmark model has had proven success over the years. Benchmark implementations based on this model continue to be widely used as engineering tools to develop new customer solutions. However, over time the public display of TPC benchmark results has diminished.

Based on the views of the TPC membership, discussions with industry analysts, and examination of adjustments made to TPC benchmarks for academic studies, we find the following reasons for why the number of official benchmark publications is diminishing:

1) TPC Enterprise benchmarks are expensive. Although the benchmark specification and any associated tool downloads are free, the remainder of the benchmark process is costly:

   a. Enterprise database application environments tend to require substantial storage, memory and processing components. Even a small TPC benchmark configuration is larger than configurations required for many other industry benchmarks.

   b. TPC Enterprise benchmarks require Roll-Your-Own applications. To run a benchmark, you either must partner with someone who has already written a benchmark implementation, or you must author a new one.

   c. TPC Enterprise benchmarks require a separately contracted audit to assure that the application specification is correctly followed for the benchmark implementation. In reality, this cost is minute in comparison to the above two items. However, it continues to be perceived as a deterrent to publishing official benchmark results in terms of both expense and time.

2) TPC Enterprise benchmarks have a rigorous set of tests and checks, either as a part of the benchmark process or a part of the audit process, that are viewed as a deterrent to producing benchmark results that can be registered with the TPC.

   a. For example, the TPC has requirements for ensuring that ACID (Atomicity, Consistency, Isolation, Durability) properties are maintained. These requirements are critical for delivery of a consumer solution, but testing them with abnormal power failures, simulated memory failures, physical removal of disks and other tests can be time consuming and expensive.

3) TPC Enterprise benchmarks require total system pricing. This is both a very positive aspect of TPC benchmarks and a deterrent to publication of benchmark results.

   a. On the positive side, the inclusion of price exposes unfair comparisons, such as configuring one system with 4 processors, 48 processor cores and 4 TB of memory and comparing it to another system having only 1 four-core processor with 64 GB of memory.

   b. However, generating a fair and accurate price for an entire configuration is a challenge for an academic study that only wants to compare two methods of delivery for a particular query function, or a storage vendor who wants to contrast their solid state and rotating storage solutions.

   c. Pricing of products is not an exact science, as it almost always depends on market forces that are not within the control of the person executing the benchmark.

   d. Pricing also proves to be a challenge for different solution delivery methods. TPC pricing requirements assume a capital purchase of dedicated computer equipment, licensing of dedicated software, and three years of maintenance costs for both. This is in stark contrast to expense-oriented costs associated with cloud based solutions, or other contracted managed operations solutions that are prevalent throughout the industry.

4) TPC benchmarks have incorrectly gained a reputation for not being publishable on the day a product or feature is announced. We include this point because, although inaccurate, the perception is that this is a deterrent to publication of TPC benchmark results.

a. The perception is that, because of TPC audit requirements and the TPC's mandatory 60-day benchmark review period, a result can only be publicized well after a product is announced.

b. The reality is that the TPC's certified benchmark auditors maintain the strictest levels of confidentiality with their clients and have shown a willingness to work with their clients to deliver timely benchmark results that are compliant with the specifications. The TPC has infrastructure in place that will allow a benchmark sponsor to prepare results well ahead of a product announcement, and have those results be known only to the sponsor and the TPC Administrator until the sponsor elects to release them. Even incomplete results can be logged with the Administrator, so that the sponsor can prepare publicity ahead of time, but can still place the final results in the TPC's database at the very last minute, with publicity commencing immediately.

5) TPC benchmarks have a reputation for not being at the forefront of computing technology.

a. Although some TPC benchmarks have existed for a long time, there are also new benchmarks that have yet to be published, so to a large degree we feel that this point is secondary to the first three items in the above list.

b. It is true, however, that benchmark development from an industry standards organization like the TPC, or SPEC (Standard Performance Evaluation Corporation), or SPC (Storage Performance Corporation) tends to take several years to complete. If something can be done to improve this process, it should be.

3   Needs for a New Benchmark Model

How does the TPC resolve these real and perceived issues while retaining the strengths of the existing TPC benchmark model? The first conclusion is not to forsake the existing model, but to enhance the TPC's offerings by introducing a new benchmark model, in parallel with the existing one. Dubbed "TPC Express", the intention is to focus on a critical subset of the database application suite, trading the ability to demonstrate absolute optimal performance for improved ease and costs of benchmarking. Fundamentally, the Enterprise model is specification-based, while the Express model will be based on predefined, executable kits that will be offered as benchmark products from the TPC.

Described further in subsequent sections of this paper, the two benchmark models are compared in the following table.

Table 1. Comparison of TPC Enterprise and TPC Express Benchmark Models

Enterprise	Express
Specification based with some TPC code	Kit based enhanced by documentation, such as a users' guide or a design document
Roll-Your-Own implementation	Out-Of-Box implementation of at least the application and perhaps also the database build routines.
Best possible optimization allowed	System tuning for "unalterable" benchmark application
Full Audit	Much self-validation, perhaps with additional post-publish review.
Price required	Price eliminated
ACID testing	ACI testing as a part of self validation
Full System Configuration	Limited configurations focused on stressing key components of the benchmark.
TPC revenues from benchmark registration	TPC revenues from license sales and potentially also benchmark registration
Substantial implementation costs	Reduced implementation costs
Ability to promote results as soon as published to the TPC	Ability to promote results as soon as published to the TPC

4   TPC Express Proposal

There are a great many things that need to be developed or enhanced within the TPC to enable development and support of TPC Express benchmark products.

- Where fairness and comparability was maintained in the Enterprise model by focusing on the delivery of specified functions in each benchmark implementation, these qualities must now be enforced as a part of the delivery of a pre-defined application.
- Where much of the compliance validation was handled by certified benchmark auditors in the Enterprise model, Express benchmarks will be validated using integrated routines that check the results of the benchmark as it is executed.
- Where existing Enterprise benchmark specifications and associated support code can be downloaded for free, the Express model will require the creation

of a license control structure that reflects the value of the work donated to generate and support the benchmark product.

- These and many other infrastructure areas are actively being developed within the TPC. In addition to the specific items necessary to support benchmarks under the Express model, the TPC is also taking a close look at the steps needed to create and approve a final benchmark product, in order to improve the time to market for novel benchmark ideas.

While these items are critical to the success of the TPC Express model, they are primarily TPC-Internal activities, and are not the primary focus of this paper. Let us assume that an Express benchmark has been created, and examine the overall life cycle of implementations of that benchmark:

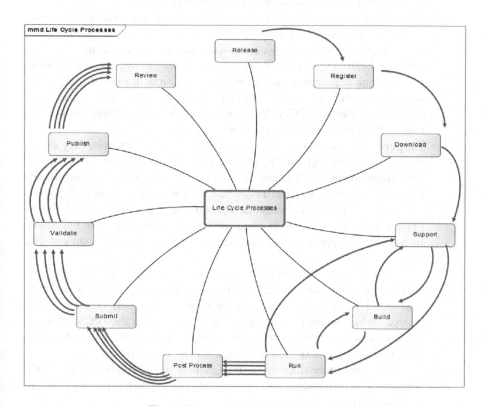

Fig. 1. Consumer Benchmark Life Cycle

- **Release:** The Benchmark is made public: In the Enterprise model, this meant that a specification and associated tooling was available for download from the TPC and the consumer could initiate development of a benchmark application. In the Express model, this will mean that a new benchmark product is being made available. The code will already have been tested in a variety of supported environments. A critical component of the development process will be to ensure that the product works in specific, declared environments. Facility needs to be provided by the TPC to allow other environments to also work with the product, but new operating environments may require some qualification process to become officially supported by the benchmark product.

- **Register:** In the Enterprise model, the most a consumer would need to do is agree to an End-User License Agreement. Because Express benchmarks will be actual products from the TPC, the registration process for these products will also include a licensing process, most likely with a nominal fee. The TPC has not completed definition of this process, but it is likely that each product will be licensed separately, that for-profit organizations will have higher fees than academic organizations, and that TPC members may receive license credit with the payment of their membership fees.

- **Download:** Upon receipt of the licensing agreement and associated payment, the TPC will make the product available to the consumer. While this could be as simple as mailing physical media, it can also be electronic download authorized through a specific license key. Although we are not detailing infrastructure requirements in this paper, this is an indication of some of the infrastructure that needs to be developed within the TPC. License and media control is new to the TPC, although it is a regular part of doing business for most of the TPC's individual members.

- **Support:** When consumers purchase a license to use a product, they expect that product to be supported by the provider. Because the TPC is a nonprofit consortium comprised of volunteers, the level of support must necessarily be limited. However, it is in the TPC's best interest to provide support, since it will help to further the benchmark product as a worthwhile tool. In the Enterprise model, this support comes from the specification, from interaction with benchmark partners such as a database vendor, and from contracts with TPC certified auditors.

  With a licensed benchmark product, the TPC needs to be prepared to provide operational and defect support for the product from within the TPC. This could be from the volunteer members of the TPC committee that created the benchmark product, or a contract with one of the TPC's affiliates, or some combination of the two. It may vary from benchmark to benchmark, but this should be transparent to the licensees of TPC products.

  As indicated in the diagram, activity associated with support, building the benchmark environment, and running the benchmark may well be an iterative process.

- **Build:** Apart from the infrastructure changes and user costs associated with acquisition of a licensed benchmark product, the benchmark build process is the first really tangible difference between the Enterprise and Express benchmark models. With the Enterprise model, the TPC often (but not always) makes available tools to generate "flat file" data that will eventually be inserted into a database which will be exercised by the benchmark.

  In the Enterprise model, how that database is defined, where each table and index will reside, how the operating system and DBMS storage management routines will access the data is both allowed to be defined by the implementer and required to be defined by the implementer. While this allows for the greatest degree of optimization, it also has a substantial implementation cost in terms of human expertise and experimentation.

With the Express model, it is expected that much of this will be predetermined. The number of options available to the benchmark implementer will be limited, but the ease of implementing the benchmark will be greatly improved. This also serves to improve confidence that the final benchmark result is valid, since the data and application build routines will be well understood.

- **Run:** The most significant difference between the benchmark models is with the preparations and measurement of the benchmark application, itself. With the Enterprise model, before initiating a benchmark run, the application has to be created. In the early years of the TPC, this application was typically written by the sponsoring hardware company. However, for much of the TPC's history, the application is written by the database partner participating in the benchmark, with enhancements applied by the hardware sponsor to match capabilities in hardware, firmware and the operating system. Regardless of the method, achieving optimal results requires an investment of time by someone who is intimately aware of the benchmark specification, the resulting application, the operating system, the firmware and the specific hardware configuration.

With the Express model, the TPC will predetermine a "typical" implementation and test it to ensure that it functions and performs as expected. While the model will not accommodate extraordinary application tuning measures to get the last few percent of performance out of the environment, the goal is that once the product is installed and the environment is built, the benchmark implementer need only press "GO" to run the benchmark.

Of course, there may still be iterative steps needed to tune the operating environment, match the target build to the system capacity, and so forth. The Express benchmark model does not eliminate the need to analyze results and optimize the environment. What it does do is contain the extent of this analysis to what would typically be required in an environment where a purchased software package is newly installed on a computer server.

To achieve this, there are new requirements placed on the development process within the TPC. The expectation that a benchmark product will run out-of-the-box means that it must be tested and proven on a wide variety of configurations prior to its release as a product.

This could also lead to a new role for TPC certified auditors. For example, if a benchmark product has been tested with two database products, and a third database wants to be included, the new company could work directly with the TPC to have their product be included in the official benchmark kit, or the TPC might provide a process where the new company can work with a certified TPC auditor to attest to the benchmark compliance of the kit adjustments needed to include the new database.

- **Post Process:** In the Enterprise model, there are three components to benchmark post processing: First, the custom kit may include some automated testing to ensure that the benchmark result is likely to be compliant. Second, the custom kit may include routines to examine the measured data for the best possible result to report. Third, the test sponsor is required to contract with a TPC-certified benchmark auditor to examine the results to attest to compliance with the benchmark requirements. This can be a substantial process, particularly for new implementations or unique hardware configurations.

  For the Express model, the expectation is that the post-processing routines will be built into the product, or perhaps explicitly described in the users guide. The intent is to have consistent post-processing for all benchmark sponsors and to have sufficient analysis that the test sponsor can be confident of the compliance of the measurement.

- **Submit:** This process may be very similar between the two models. The TPC already has a sophisticated mechanism for submission of results, including an option to immediately register and publish a complete result, an option to register a complete result with delayed publication (keeping the result confidential until the delay expires) and an option to pre-register an incomplete result (to prepare for future publicity) with the intent to make the result complete prior to its public release. Some adjustments to this process may be needed, but the basic functions are already sound for both the Enterprise and Express models.

  As soon as the submission process is complete, the benchmark sponsor may begin publicizing the results. This is true in the current Enterprise model and is expected to be true in the Express model. It has been suggested that publicity ought to be allowed even without a formal submission. It is clear that some academic studies will not require submission of benchmark results. However, if a competitive comparison is to be made with existing registered benchmark results, it seems reasonable to require submission of a result prior to the comparison becoming public. The TPC has made it sufficiently easy to submit a result. Results that are not submitted through the TPC's process should not be considered to be comparable to results that have gone through the full process.

- **Validate:** This step is largely transparent to the benchmark sponsor who is submitting the result. In the Enterprise model, the staff at the office of the TPC Administrator check to ensure that all necessary components are present. With the use of TPC-certified benchmark auditors, there is a high confidence that the results are compliant with the benchmark requirements.

  With the Express model, the TPC may choose to conduct additional validation of the result prior to publication. If additional validation is needed, it must be conducted in a timely manner, based on the potential need to publicize the result.

- **Publish:** As discussed earlier, the actual publication of a result can be controlled entirely by the benchmark sponsor. If results are submitted that are believed to be compliant with the benchmark rules, they are published on the date of the submitter's choosing. This will be true for both Enterprise and Express models.

- **Review:** The current Enterprise model has a 60-day review period for all results. The result is presumed to be correct (as attested to by a TPC-certified benchmark auditor) and may be publicized during the review period. A similar review period is likely for the Express model, although there will be high confidence in the compliance of the result, since the benchmark application will be well understood.

5   Existing Benchmark Models in the Industry

One might ask "Why not just join SPEC?" Certainly the Standard Performance Evaluation Corporation (SPEC) has seen substantial success with many of its benchmarks, and the TPC Express model has some distinct similarities to many aspects of SPEC benchmark products. Furthermore, SPEC already has groups that focus on high performance computing, workstation and graphics computing, and general server computing – so why not add a group that focuses on database computing?

Examination of SPEC's public documentation regarding their benchmarks and the procedures associated with them was certainly one of the areas of research that led to the development of the Express proposal. SPEC has developed a very successful product development and delivery system, and some of their benchmarks have been extremely popular. On the other hand, there are also some SPEC benchmark products that have not seen a publication on the SPEC site for two or more years. It is only practical to assume that simply becoming a part of the SPEC organization is not a guarantee of having a successful benchmark product.

It is worthwhile examining some of SPEC's success stories. Of the current or near-current SPEC benchmark products, the three with the greatest number of publishes are SPECjbb2005, SPECpower_ssj2008 and the SPECcpu2006 suite. For the first two quarters of 2013, SPECpower_ssj2008 had 19 publishes, with a current lifetime total of 440. SPECjbb2005 was recently replaced with SPECjbb2013. In it's final two quarters as a current benchmark, it had 39 publications and it enjoyed a lifetime publish list of 746 results. Although the SPECcpu2006 suite is actually 4 benchmarks, it is almost astounding that in the first two quarters of 2013 it had 729 published results – an indication that one should not be surprised to learn that the lifetime publication list totaled 4,391 up to July 2013.

One must ask "What are the components that generated these levels of success?" We believe there are five key qualities, of which the first three are the most important:

1)   The benchmark products have an order/delivery/execution/validation process that is easily understood and managed by the end user. Providing a similar process is the focus of the portion of the TPC Express model that has been described earlier in this paper.

2) The benchmark products focus on key components of computing in the industry that are deemed to be important by those interested in running the benchmarks. It is not critical that these key components be "new and novel." The SPECcpu suite focuses a great deal on compiler technology and optimization – something that has been with the industry since computers shifted from interpretive to compiled programs. TPC Enterprise benchmarks clearly already focus on key areas in the industry - - All businesses require enterprise database applications to run. However, just satisfying this requirement, without the others in this list, is insufficient.

3) The three SPEC products listed above fit on servers of almost any size. Although there can be substantial memory and processor requirements to achieve optimal performance, all three benchmarks can be run on systems with minimal storage and can execute on both small and large processor/memory configurations. This makes the benchmarks affordable for measurement on many configurations. This is in contrast to current TPC Enterprise benchmarks, which require very robust configurations to execute properly. To achieve this configuration economy typically requires a compromise in the "completeness" of the benchmark application. It is important that the functions tested satisfy item 2, above, but it is a reasonable trade-off to say that the benchmark need not test "every" function in the business model being emulated by the benchmark.

4) The benchmarks are attractive to the academic community. This is really a result of the first three items in the list – relatively easy to use, focusing on an area of interest, and capable of being measured on a wide spectrum of configurations, including inexpensive ones. The additional requirements for the academic community are the ability to make adjustments, if needed, for specific experiments and having a pool of existing data to compare to. Although there will be cases when fully compliant benchmark results are not generated by the academic community, because of the nature of the experiments conducted, there will be a much higher potential for academic results to be fully comparable to official results if the first three items in this list are satisfied.

5) The existing pool of results attracts interest in generating additional results. Also a result of the first three items in the list, with a symbiotic relation to the fourth item. As more results are generated, it is more likely that more results will be generated.

Although some additional actions may be required to encourage the fourth and fifth items, the key areas to examine for TPC Express are the first three in the list. The first item is an aspect of most SPEC benchmarks, although the degree of ease varies. SPEC benchmarks that are not published as heavily tend to fall short in either the second or third category. TPC Enterprise benchmarks tend to fall short in the first and third. The goal of TPC Express must be to develop both processes and benchmarks that satisfy all of these.

6   Meeting the Challenge

The intent of the TPC Express model is to develop a suite of benchmarks that are complimentary to the TPC Enterprise model and that satisfy the perceived needs discussed here. It is hoped that the Express model can be applied to data processing areas that have yet to be explored in TPC benchmarks.

Although several benchmarks are desired, there must always be a first instance of any new concept. The clear goal is to ensure that all three of the key items listed in the previous section are satisfied in this first Express product.

To facilitate development of the Express model and speed delivery of the first benchmark, a member company has volunteered to contribute substantial portions of their TPC-E benchmark kit and to work with members of the TPC to alter the kit to create a new benchmark. The benchmark will likely have some similar characteristics to TPC-E, but will be substantively different and will produce results that are not comparable to TPC-E results.

The base kit has been used by the member company and their partners to measure and analyze TPC-E results in the TPC Enterprise space. It includes many of the characteristics discussed in section 4 of this paper, although some enhancement may be required to satisfy all of the delivery and execution characteristics that are needed. In doing so, the kit will satisfy the first of the three critical needs listed in the previous section.

The database build and benchmark execution characteristics will be significantly different from those of TPC-E, both to ensure that the new benchmark is not comparable to TPC-E and to help satisfy some of the requirements for ease of measurement and validation. As these adjustments and enhancements are made, the TPC will be mindful of the second major requirement – to continue to focus on key functions that are of interest to those who conduct benchmarks and their audiences.

The third critical point is to develop a benchmark that can be run on an affordable configuration. In this regard, one of the key decisions that have been made is to target an active data volume for the benchmark that will fit in memory. Much prototype experimentation is required to be able to deliver this, but the current goal is to deliver a benchmark that will essentially fit in 256 GB for the processing power provided by one processor (one populated processor socket). Through the process of prototyping the new benchmark, it may be possible to drop this target to a much smaller amount. The memory target will not preclude executing on smaller amounts of memory, although smaller systems will suffer in performance. It will mean that configurations with massive storage subsystems will not be required for running the benchmark.

7   Opportunities for Contribution

There are many areas in data processing that are not currently covered in any industry standard benchmark. The TPC believes that the new TPC Express benchmark model will open opportunities for new benchmark areas to be explored. The TPC welcomes active participation in this endeavor – from full TPC members, associate TPC members, and those who have not yet joined the TPC, but have an interest in expanding the breadth of industry standard data processing benchmarks.

This is not a short-term proposal, but one that the TPC expects to be in place for many years. As new benchmark prototypes are generated for cloud computing, big data, data transformation, analytics, data approximations, symbiotic transactions, and so on and so on - - the opportunity exists to work with the TPC to formalize the application into a meaningful benchmark product that can help to advance the industry.

8   Summary

The TPC Express benchmark model is an exciting development for the TPC, for TPC members and for the data processing industry. The TPC is actively working on the infrastructure needed to support such a model and is simultaneously working on the first Express-model benchmark. This first instance will be a fairly extensive remodeling of an existing TPC Enterprise benchmark – both to speed the delivery of the first Express benchmark and to aid in the development of the necessary support infrastructure.

The TPC expects and welcomes ideas to build on this concept, to deliver new benchmarks that are of use to the industry, academia and consumers and that focus on a spectrum of important data processing features.

References

1. Transaction Processing Performance Council: "TPC Policies, Revision 5.26", http://www.tpc.org/information/about/documentation/doc.asp
2. Standard Performance Evaluation Corporation: "SPEC OSG Policies", http://www.spec.org/osg/policy.html
3. Huppler, K.: The Art of Building a Good Benchmark. In: Nambiar, R., Poess, M. (eds.) TPCTC 2009. LNCS, vol. 5895, pp. 18–30. Springer, Heidelberg (2009)
4. Internal research from InfoSizing Corporation and TPC Steering Committee

TPC-H Analyzed: Hidden Messages and Lessons Learned from an Influential Benchmark

Peter Boncz[1], Thomas Neumann[2], and Orri Erling[3]

[1] CWI, Amsterdam, The Netherlands
boncz@cwi.nl
[2] Technical University Munich, Germany
neumann@in.tum.de
[3] Openlink Software, United Kingdom
oerling@openlinksw.com

Abstract. The TPC-D benchmark was developed almost 20 years ago, and even though its current existence as TPC-H could be considered superseded by TPC-DS, one can still learn from it. We focus on the technical level, summarizing the challenges posed by the TPC-H workload as we now understand them, which we call "choke points". We identify 28 different such choke points, grouped into six categories: Aggregation Performance, Join Performance, Data Access Locality, Expression Calculation, Correlated Subqueries and Parallel Execution. On the meta-level, we make the point that the rich set of choke-points found in TPC-H sets an example on how to design future DBMS benchmarks.[1]

1 Introduction

Good benchmark design starts with a use case that is recognizable and understandable, and where the data being stored as well as query and update workloads being posed, resemble those of a wider class of data management problems faced by IT practitioners (and more, see [1]). However, basing a benchmark solely on "real-life" data management scenarios, data-sets and query logs will not necessarily lead to an interesting benchmark, for instance because such real-world examples characterize what technology can do now, not what it could do in the future. Moreover, the value in a benchmark is not only in allowing data management practitioners to test different technologies and compare them quantitatively, but also in stimulating *technological advances*.

In the LDBC (Linked Data Benchmark Council) project, these authors are currently pursuing the design of new benchmarks that will stimulate technological advance in graph (and RDF) data management. For this purpose, LDBC follows a dual design track where on the one hand a Technical User Community (TUC) consisting of data management technology practitioners contribute data-sets and workloads, but on the other hand, technology experts both from industry and academic database research provide technical guidance on what we

---

[1] Partially supported by EU project LDBC (FP7-317548), see http://ldbc.eu

R. Nambiar and M. Poess (Eds.): TPCTC 2013, LNCS 8391, pp. 61–76, 2014.
© Springer International Publishing Switzerland 2014

call "choke points", that should be embedded in these new benchmarks. Choke points are those technological challenges underlying a benchmark, whose resolution will significantly improve the performance of a product.

This paper was written with a dual motivation: (i) to use the by now well-understood TPC-H benchmark to illustrate examples of what we understand "choke points" to be, and use TPC-H as an example of a benchmark that contains a rich set of these, and (ii) as an overview and reference for analytical data management practitioners to better understand the TPC-H workload itself; concentrating collected wisdom on this benchmark in a single place.

We do not dispute that TPC-H, which is almost 20 years old, could by some be regarded as superseded (e.g. by TPC-DS). The purpose of this paper is *not* to criticize TPC-H or suggest improvements as has been done elsewhere [2], but rather to describe what TPC-H is. We would appreciate any future benchmark to be at least as rich in relevant technical challenges as TPC-D was in 1995.

2   TPC-H Choke Point Analysis

Table 1 contains the summary of our choke point classification, which in the remainder of this paper will be discussed point-by-point.

2.1   Aggregation Performance

Aggregations occur in all TPC-H queries, hence performance of group-by and aggregation is quite important.

CP1.1: Ordered Aggregation. Aggregation implementations typically use a hash-table to store the group-by keys in. This is an efficient method, because hash-lookup (with a properly sized hash-table) has constant lookup cost. Hash-aggregation does run into performance deterioration when the amount of distinct group-by keys is large. When the hash-table will no longer fit the various CPU cache levels, cache and TLB misses will make the lookup more costly CPU-wise. With even more distinct keys, one may get to the situation that the hash-table cannot be kept in RAM anymore. Here a *spilling* hash aggregation would be needed, that first hash-partitions the tuple stream to different files based on the hash value, and then aggregates the individual files inside RAM one-at-a-time. Spilling hash aggregations are not obviously superior to other methods, such as those based on creating a B-tree or, more plausibly, those based on sorting (external memory sort). In case the group-by keys arrive in sorted order, or actually much more generally, if all equal group-by keys *appear consecutively* in the stream, one should employ ordered aggregation instead of hash aggregation.

These approaches can even be mixed, e.g., using repetitive grouped execution of hash-aggregation, or using hash-based early aggregation in a sort-based spilling approach. Therefore the key challenge is detecting which situation applies, which depends both on the available hardware and the query characteristics. Related to this, the query optimizer has to infer the correct intermediate result cardinalities, which is relatively simple for most TPC-H query constructs, but challenging for group-by expressions.

Table 1. TPC-H Choke Point (CP) classification, and CP impact per query (white=light, gray=medium, black=strong)

Q1	Q2	Q3	Q4	Q5	Q6	Q7	Q8	Q9	Q10	Q11	Q12	Q13	Q14	Q15	Q16	Q17	Q18	Q19	Q20	Q21	Q22

CP1 Aggregation Performance. Performance of aggregate calculations.

CP1.1 QEXE: Ordered Aggregation.
CP1.2 QOPT: Interesting Orders.
CP1.3 QOPT: Small Group-by Keys (array lookup).
CP1.4 QEXE: Dependent Group-By Keys (removal of).

CP2 Join Performance. Voluminous joins, with or without selections.

CP2.1 QEXE: Large Joins (out-of-core).
CP2.2 QEXE: Sparse Foreign Key Joins (bloom filters).
CP2.3 QOPT: Rich Join Order Optimization.
CP2.4 QOPT: Late Projection (column stores).

CP3 Data Access Locality. Non-full-scan access to (correlated) table data.

CP3.1 STORAGE: Columnar Locality (favors column storage).
CP3.2 STORAGE: Physical Locality by Key (clustered index, partitioning).
CP3.3 QOPT: Detecting Correlation (ZoneMap,MinMax,multi-attribute histograms).

CP4 Expression Calculation. Efficiency in evaluating (complex) expressions.

CP4.1 Raw Expression Arithmetic.
CP4.1a QEXE: Arithmetic Operation Performance.
CP4.1b QEXE: Overflow Handling (in arithmetic operations).
CP4.1c QEXE: Compressed Execution.
CP4.1d QEXE: Interpreter Overhead (vectorization; CPU/GPU/FPGA JIT compil.).
CP4.2 Complex Boolean Expressions in Joins and Selections.
CP4.2a QOPT: Common Subexpression Elimination (CSE).
CP4.2b QOPT: Join-Dependent Expression Filter Pushdown.
CP4.2c QOPT: Large IN Clauses (invisible join).
CP4.2d QEXE: Evaluation Order in Conjunctions and Disjunctions.
CP4.3 String Matching Performance.
CP4.3a QOPT: Rewrite LIKE(X%) into a Range Query.
CP4.3b QEXE: Raw String Matching Performance (e.g. using SSE4.2).
CP4.3c QEXE: Regular Expression Compilation (JIT/FSA generation).

CP5 Correlated Subqueries. Efficiently handling dependent subqueries.

CP5.1 QOPT: Flattening Subqueries (into join plans).
CP5.2 QOPT: Moving Predicates into a Subquery.
CP5.3 QEXE: Overlap between Outer- and Subquery.

CP6 Parallelism and Concurrency. Making use of parallel computing resources.

CP6.1 QOPT: Query Plan Parallelization.
CP6.2 QEXE: Workload Management.
CP6.3 QEXE: Result Re-use.

CP1.2: Interesting Orders. Apart from clustered indexes providing key order, other operators also preserve or even induce tuple orderings. Sort-based operators create new orderings, typically the probe-side of a hash join conserves its order, etc. For instance TPC-H Q3,4,18 join ORDERS and LINEITEM, followed by aggregation grouped-by on o_orderkey. If the tuple order of ORDERS is conserved by the join, ordered aggregation is applicable. This is not to say that it is always best to use the join order with ORDERS on the probe side and LINEITEM on the build side (in hash-join terms), but *if* this is chosen then the ordered aggregation benefit should be reaped. A similar opportunity arises in Q21 with a join between SUPPLIER and LINEITEM, and grouped-by on s_suppkey. These are an examples of *interesting order* handling where the query optimization space should take multiple orders into account [3] (i.e. choosing a particular join methods leads to lower aggregation cost, subsequently).

CP1.3: Small Group-By Keys. Q1 computes eight aggregates: a count, four sums and three averages. Group-by keys are l_returnflag, l_linestatus, with just four occurring value combinations. This points to a possibility to optimize a special case of group-by. Namely, if all group-by expressions can be represented as integers in a small range, one can use an array to keep the aggregate totals by position, rather then keeping them in a hash-table. This can be extended to multiple group-by keys if their concatenated integer representation is still "small". In case of Q1, the group-by attributes are single-characters strings (VARCHAR(1)) which can be stored as an integer e.g. holding the Unicode value.

CP1.4: Dependent Group-By Keys. Q10 has a group-by on c_custkey *and* the columns c_comment, c_address, n_name, c_phone, c_acctbal, c_name. The amount of data processed is large, since the query involves a one-year ORDERS and LINEITEM join towards CUSTOMER. Given that c_custkey is the primary key of CUSTOMER, the query optimizer can deduce that its value *functionally determines* the columns c_comment, c_address, n_name, c_phone, c_acctbal, c_name. As a result, the aggregation operator should have the ability to exclude certain group-by attributes from key matching: this can greatly reduce the CPU cost and (cache) memory footprint of such an operator. This opportunity arises in many other queries that have an aggregation that includes a tuple identity (denoted #) in addition to other columns that are functionally determined by it:

Q3 #o → o_shippriority, o_orderdate
Q4 #o → o_orderpriority
Q10 #c → c_comment, c_address, n_name, c_phone, c_acctbal, c_name
Q13 #c → count(*)
Q18 #c,#l → l_quantity, o_totalprice, o_orderdate, c_name
Q20 #s → s_address, s_name
Q21 #s → s_name

Even though declaring keys is optional in the rules of TPC-H, functional dependency exploitation in aggregation is a clear argument why one would do so. An additional argument is execution optimization that can be performed when executing N:1 foreign key joins: knowing that exactly one value will be added to an intermediate result record, allows to lower CPU effort (breaking off hash-table search after the first hit) and to avoid intermediate data copying, which is needed if a join "blows up" an intermediate result in case of a 1:N join.

In this sense, it is noteworthy that the EXASOL TPC-H implementations do not declare (foreign) keys, but add a "foreign key check" query set to the load phase; it is understood that a side effect of this may be the detection of these (foreign) key constraints. This might avoid the only drawback of declaring constraints: namely the obligation to check these in the refresh queries.

2.2   Join Performance

CP2.1: Large Joins. Joins are the most costly relational operators, and there has been a lot of research and different algorithmic variants proposed. Generally speaking, the basic choice is between hash- and index-based join methods. It is no longer assumed that hash-based methods are always superior to index-based methods; the choice between the two depends on the system implementation of these methods, as well as on the physical database design: in general, index-based join methods are used in those situations where the data is stored in an index with a key of which the join key is a prefix. For the cost model, whether the index is clustered or unclustered makes a large difference in systems relying on I/O; but (as by now often is the case) if the TPC-H workload hot-set fits into the RAM, the unclustered penalty may be only moderate.

Q9 and Q18 are the queries with the largest joins *without* selection predicates between the largest tables ORDERS and LINEITEM. The heaviest case is Q9, which essentially joins it also with PARTSUPP, PART and SUPPLIER with only a 1 in 17 selection on PART. The join graph has the largest table LINEITEM joining with both ORDERS and PARTSUPP. It may be possible to get locality on the former join, using either clustered indexing or table partitioning; this will create a merge-join like pattern, or a partitioned join where only matching partitions need to be joined. However, using these methods, the latter join towards the still significantly large PARTSUPP table will not have locality. This lack of locality causes large resource consumption, thus Q9 can be seen as the query that tests for out-of-core join methods (e.g. spilling hash-joins). In TPC-H, by configuring the test machine with sufficient RAM, typically disk spilling can be avoided, avoiding its high performance penalty. In the case of parallel database systems, lack of join locality will cause unavoidable network communication, which quickly can become a performance bottleneck. Parallel database systems can only avoid such communication by replicating the PARTSUPP, PART and SUPPLIER tables on all nodes – a strategy which increases memory pressure and disk footprint, but which is not penalized by extra maintenance cost, since the TPC-H refresh queries do not modify these particular tables.

For specific queries, usage of special join types may be beneficial. For example, Q13 can be accelerated by the GroupJoin operator [4], which combines the outer join with the aggregation and thus avoids building the same hash table twice.

CP2.2: Sparse Foreign Key Joins. Joins occur in all TPC-H queries except Q1,6; and they are invariably over N:1 or 1:N foreign key relationships. In contrast to Q9 and Q18, the joins in all other queries typically involve selections; very frequently the :1 side of the join is restricted by predicates. This in turn means that tuples from the N: side, instead of finding exactly one join partner, often find no partner at all. In TPC-H it is typical that the resulting *join hit-ratios* are below 1 in 10, and often much lower. This makes it beneficial for systems to implement a *bloom filter* test inside the join [5]; since this will eliminate the great majority of the join lookups in a CPU-wise cheap way, at low RAM investments. For example, in case of VectorWise, bloom filters are created on-the-fly if a hash-join experiences a low hit ratio, and make the PARTSUPP-PART join in Q2 six times faster, accelerating Q2 two-fold overall.

Bloom filters created for a join should be tested as early as possible, potentially before the join, even moving it down into the probing scan. This way, the CPU work is reduced early, and column stores may further benefit from reduced decompression cost in the scan and potentially also less I/O, if full blocks are skipped [6]. Bloom filter pushdown is furthermore essential in MPP systems in case of such low hit-ratio joins. The communication protocol between the nodes should allow a join to be preceded by a bloom filter exchange; before sending probe keys over the network in a communicating join, each local node first checks the bloom filter to see if it can match at all. In such way, bloom filters allow to significantly bring down network bandwidth usage, helping scalability.

CP2.3: Rich Join Order Optimization. TPC-H has queries which join up to eight tables with widely varying cardinalities. The execution times of different join orders differ by orders of magnitude. Therefore, finding an efficient join order is important, and, in general, requires enumeration of all join orders, e.g., using dynamic programming. The enumeration is complicated by operators that are not freely reorderable like semi, anti, and outer joins. Because of this difficulty most join enumeration algorithms do not enumerate all possible plans, and therefore can miss the optimal join order. One algorithm that can properly handle semi-, anti-, and outer-joins was developed by IBM for DB2 [7]. Moerkotte and Neumann [8] presented a more general algorithm based on hypergraphs, which supports all relational operators and, using hyperedges, supports join predicates between more than two tables.

CP2.4: Late Projection. In column stores, queries where certain columns are only used late in the plan, can typically do better by omitting them from the original table scans, to fetch them later by row-id with a separate scan operator which is joined to the intermediate query result. Late projection does have a trade-off involving locality, since late in the plan the tuples may be in a different order, and scattered I/O in terms of tuples/second is much more expensive than sequential I/O. Late projection specifically makes sense in queries where the late use of these columns happens at a moment where the amount of tuples involves has been considerably reduced; for example after an aggregation with only few unique group-by keys, or a top-N operator. There are multiple queries in TPC-H that have such pattern, the most clear examples being Q5 and Q10.

A lightweight form of late projection can also be applied to foreign key joins, scanning for the probe side first only the join keys, and only in case there is a match, fetching the remaining columns (as mentioned in the bloom filter discussion). In case of sparse foreign key joins, this will lead to reduced column decompression CPU work, and potentially also less I/O – if full blocks can be skipped.

2.3   Data Access Locality

A popular data storage technique in data warehousing is the *materialized view*. Even though the TPC-H workload consists of multiple query runs, where the 22 TPC-H queries are instrumented with different parameters, it is possible to create very small materialized views that basically contain the parameterized answers to the queries. Oracle issued in 1998 the One Million Dollar Challenge, for anyone who could demonstrate that Microsoft SQLserver 7.0 was not 100 times slower than Oracle when running TPC-D; exploiting the fact that Oracle had introduced materialized views before SQLserver did. Since materialized views essentially turn the decision support queries of TPC-D into pre-calculated result-lookups, the benchmark no longer tested ad-hoc query processing capabilities. This led to the split of TPC-D into TPC-R (R for Reporting, now retired, where materialized views were allowed), and TPC-H, where materialized views were outlawed. As such, even though materialized views are an important feature in data warehousing, TPC-H does not test their functionality.

CP3.1: Columnar Locality. The original TPC-D benchmark did not allow the use of vertical partitioning. However, in the past decade TPC-H has been allowing systems that uniformly vertically partition all tables ("column stores"). Columnar storage is popular as it accelerates many analytical workloads, without relying on a DBA to e.g. carefully choose materialized views or clustered indexes. As such, it is considered a more "robust" technique. The main advantage of columnar storage is that queries only need to access those columns that actually are used in a query. Since no TPC-H query is of the form SELECT * FROM .., this benefit is present in all queries. Given that roughly half of the TPC-H data volume is in the columns l_comment and o_comment (in VectorWise), which are very infrequently accessed, one realizes the benefit is even larger than the average fraction of columns used by a query.

Not only do column-stores eliminate unneeded I/O, they also employ effective columnar compression, and are best combined with an efficient query compiler or execution engine. In fact, both the TPC-H top-scores for cluster and single-server hardware platforms in the years 2010-2013 have been in the hands of columnar products (EXASOL and VectorWise).

CP3.2: Physical Locality by Key. The TPC-H tables ORDERS and LINEITEM contain a few date columns, that are correlated by the data generator:

 - l_shipdate = o_orderdate + random[1:121],
 - l_commitdate = o_orderdate + random[30:90], and
 - l_receiptdate = l_shipdate + random[1:30].

In Q3, there is a selection with lower bound (LO) on l_shipdate and a higher bound (HI) on o_orderdate. Given the above, one could say that o_orderdate is thereby restricted on the day range [LO-121:HI]. Similar bounds follow for *any* of the date columns in LINEITEM. The combination of a lower and higher bound from *different* tables in Q3 is an extreme case, but in Q4,5,8,10,12 there are range restrictions on one date column, that carry over to a date restriction to the other side of the ORDERS-LINEITEM join.

Clustered Indexes. It follows that storing the ORDERS relation in a clustered index on o_orderdate and LINEITEM on a clustered index on any of its date columns; in combination with e.g. unclustered indexes to enforce their primary keys, leads to joins that can have high data locality. Not only will a range restriction save I/O on both scans feeding into the join, but in a nested-loops index join the cursor will be moving in date order through both tables quasi-sequentially; even if the access is by the orderkey via an unclustered index lookup. Such an unclustered index could easily be RAM resident and thus fast to access.

In Q3,4,5,8,10,12 the date range selections take respectively 2,3,12,12,3,12 out of 72 months. Typically this 1 in 6 to 1 in 36 selection fraction on the ORDERS table is propagable to the large LINEITEM table, providing very significant benefits. In Q12 the direction is reverted: the range predicate is on l_receiptdate and can be propagated to ORDERS (similar actually happens in Q7, here through l_shipdate). Even though this locality automatically emerges during joins if ORDERS and LINEITEM both are stored in a clustered index with a date key, the best plan might not be found by the optimizer if it is not aware of the correlation. Microsoft SQLserver specifically offers the DATE_CORRELATION_OPTIMIZATION setting that tells the optimizer to keep correlated statistics.

Table Partitioning. Range-partitioning is often used in practice on a time dimension, in which case it provides support for so-called *data life-cycle management*. That is, a data warehouse may keep the X last months of data, which means that every month the oldest archived month must be removed from the dataset. Using range-partitioning, such can be efficiently achieved by range-partitioning the data per month, dropping the oldest partition. However, the refresh workload of TPC-H does not fit this pattern, since its deletes and inserts are not time-correlated. The benefit from table partitioning in TPC-H is hence *partition pruning*, which both can happen in handling selection queries (by not scanning those partitions that cannot contain results, given a selection predicate) and in joins between tables that are partitioned on the primary and foreign keys.

Data correlation could be exploited in partitioning as well, even respecting the TPC-H rule that no index creation directive (or any other DDL) would mention multiple tables. For example, for range-partitioned tables it is relatively easy to automatically maintain for all declared foreign key joins to another partitioned table a *pruning bitmap* for each partition, that tells with which partitions on the other side the join result is empty. Such a pruning bitmap would steer join partition pruning and could be cheaply maintained as a side effect of foreign-key constraint checking.

CP3.3: Detecting Correlation. While the TPC-H schema rewards creating these clustered indexes, in case of LINEITEM the question then is which of the three date columns to use as key. One could say that l_shipdate is used more often (in Q6,15,20) than `l_receiptdate` (just Q12), but in fact it should not matter which column is used, as range-propagation between correlated attributes of the same table is relatively easy. One way is through creation of multi-attribute histograms after detection of attribute correlation, such as suggested by the CORDS work in DB2 [9]. Another method is to use small materialized aggregates [10] or even simpler MinMax indexes (VectorWise) or zone-maps (Netezza), The latter data structures maintain the MIN and MAX value of each column, for a limited number of zones in the table. As these MIN/MAX are rough bounds only (i.e. the bounds are allowed to be wider than the real data), maintenance that only widens the ranges on need, can be done immediately by any query without transactional locking.

With MinMax indexes, range-predicates on any column can be translated into qualifying tuple position ranges. If an attribute value is correlated with tuple position, this reduces the area to scan roughly equally to predicate selectivity. For instance, even if the `LINEITEM` is clustered on `l_receiptdate`, this will still find tight tuple position ranges for predicates on `l_shipdate` (and vice versa).

2.4   Expression Calculation

TPC-H tests expression calculation performance, in three areas:

- **CP4.1: raw expression arithmetic.**
- **CP4.2: complex boolean expressions in joins and selections.**
- **CP4.3: string matching performance.**

We elaborate on different technical aspects of these in the following.

Q1 calculates a full price, and then computes various aggregates.[2] The large amount of tuples to go through in Q1, which selects 99% of `LINEITEM`, makes it worthwhile to optimize its many arithmetic calculations.

CP4.1a: Arithmetic Operator Performance. According to the TPC-H rules, it is allowed to represent decimals as 64-bits doubles, yet this will lead to limited SIMD opportunities only (4-way in 256-bit AVX). Moreover, this approach to decimals is likely to be unacceptable for business users of database systems, because of the rounding errors that inevitably appear on "round" decimal numbers. Another alternative for decimal storage is to use variable-length numerical strings, allowing to store arbitrarily precise numbers; however in that case arithmetic will be very slow, and this would very clearly show in e.g. Q1.

---

[2] **Some notes on Q1.**

Compared to Q6, the only other non-join query, the amount of computation done in Q1 is larger, making it more likely to be CPU-bound than Q6.

Also, Q1 trivially parallelizes: the aggregate result is very small, so the plan can be run on many cores (or machines) in parallel without need for synchronization or result communication of any significance. This makes Q1 the only query that allows to make back-of-the-envelope estimates of the computational power of a database engine even across systems and platforms and database sizes, since normalization to a single-core and scale is relatively straightforward.

A common and efficient implementation for decimals is to store integers containing the number without dot. The TPC-H spec states that the decimal type should support the range [-9,999,999,999.99: 9,999,999,999.99] with increments of 0.01. That way, the stored integer would be the decimal value times 100 and 42-bits of precision are required for TPC-H decimals, hence a 32-bits integer is too small but a 64-bits integer suffices. Decimal arithmetic can thus rely on integer arithmetic, which is machine-supported and even SIMD can be exploited.

It is not uncommon for database systems to keep statistics on the minimum and maximum values in each table column. The columns used in Q1 exhibit the following ranges: l_extendedprice[0.00:100000.00], l_quantity[1.00:50.00], l_discount[0.00:0.10] and l_tax[0.00:0.08]. This means that irrespective of how data is physically stored (columnar systems would typically compress the data), during query processing these columns could be represented in byte-aligned integers of 32, 16, 8 and 8 bits respectively. The expression (1-l_discount) using an 8-bits representation can thus be handled by SIMD subtraction, processing 32 tuples per 256-bits AVX instruction. However, the subsequent multiplication with l_extendedprice requires to convert the result of (1-l_discount) to 32-bits integers, still allowing 256-bits SIMD multiplication to process 8 tuples per instruction. This highlights that in order to exploit SIMD well, it pays to keep data represented as long as possible in as small as possible integers (stored column-wise). Aligning all values on the widest common denominator (the 32-bits extendedprice) would hurt the performance of four out of the six arithmetic operations in our example Q1; making them a factor 4 slower.

While SIMD instructions are most easily applied in normal projection calculations, it is also possible to use SIMD for updating aggregate totals. In aggregations with group-by keys, this can be done if there are multiple COUNT or SUM operations on data items of the same width, which then should not be stored column-wise but rather row-wise in adjacent fields [11].

CP4.1b: Overflow Handling. Arithmetic overflow handling is a seldom covered topic in database research literature, yet it is a SQL requirement. Overflow checking using if-then-else tests for each operation causes CPU overhead, because it is extra computation. Therefore there is an advantage to ensuring that overflow cannot happen, by combining knowledge of data ranges and the proper choice of data types. In such cases, explicit overflow check codes that would be more costly than the arithmetic itself can be omitted, and SIMD can be used. The 32-bits multiplication l_extendedprice*(1-l_discount), i.e. [0.00:100000.00]*[0.00:0.90] results in the more precise value range [0.0000: 90000.0000] represented by cardinals up to 900 million; hence 32-bits integers still cannot overflow in this case. Thus, testing can be omitted for this expression.

CP4.1c: Compressed Execution. Compressed execution allows certain predicates to be evaluated without decompressing the data it operates on, saving CPU effort. The poster-child use case of compressed execution is aggregation on RLE compressed numerical data [12], however this is only possible in aggregation queries without group-by. This only occurs in TPC-H Q6, but does not apply there either given that the involved l_extendedprice column is unlikely to be

RLE compressed. As such, the only opportunities for compressed execution in TPC-H are in column vs. constant comparisons that appear in selection clauses; here the largest benefits are achieved by executing a VARCHAR comparison on dictionary-compressed data, such that it becomes an integer comparison.

CP4.1d: Interpreter Overhead. The large amount of expression calculation in Q1 penalizes slow interpretative (tuple-at-a-time) query engines. Various solutions to interpretation have been developed, such as using FPGA hardware (KickFire), GPU hardware (ParStream), vectorized execution (VectorWise) and Just-In-Time (JIT) compilation (HyPer, ParAccel); typically beating tuple-at-a-time interpreters by orders of magnitude in Q1.

CP4.2a: Common Subexpression Elimination. A basic technique helpful in multiple TPC-H queries is common subexpression elimination (CSE). In Q1, this reduces the six arithmetic operations to be calculated to just four. CSE should also recognize that two of the average aggregates can be derived afterwards by dividing a SUM by the COUNT, both also computed in Q1.

CP4.2b: Join-Dependent Expression Filter Pushdown. In Q7 and Q19 there are complex join conditions which depend on both sides of the join. In Q7, which is a join query that unites customer-nations (cn) via orders, lineitems, and suppliers to supplier-nations (sn), and on top of this it selects:
(sn.n_name = '[NATION1]' AND cn.n_name = '[NATION2]') OR
(sn.n_name = '[NATION2]' AND cn.n_name = '[NATION1]').

Hence TPC-H rewards optimizers that can analyze complex join conditions which cannot be pushed below the join, but still derive *filters* from such join conditions. For instance, if the plan would start by joining CUSTOMER to NATION, it could immediate filter the latter scan with the condition:
(cn.n_name = '[NATION1]' OR cn.n_name = '[NATION2]')

This will reduce data volume by a factor 12.5. A similar technique can be used on the disjunctive complex expression in Q19. The general strategy is to take the union of the individual table predicates appearing in the disjunctive condition, and filter on this in the respective scan. A further optimization is to rewrite the NATION scans as subqueries in the FROM clause:

```
(SELECT (CASE n_name = '[NATION1]' THEN 1 ELSE 0 END) AS nation1,
        (CASE n_name = '[NATION2]' THEN 1 ELSE 0 END) AS nation2
 FROM nation WHERE n_name = '[NATION1]' or n_name = '[NATION2]') cn
```
   And subsequently test the join condition as:
(sn.nation1=1 AND cn.nation2=1) OR (sn.nation2=1 AND cn.nation1=1)

The rationale for the above is that integer tests (executed on the large join result) are faster than string equality. A rewrite like this may not be needed for (column store) systems that use *compressed execution*, i.e. the ability to execute certain predicates in certain operators without decompressing data [13].

CP 4.2c: Large IN Clauses. In Q19, Q16 and Q22 (and also Q12) there are IN predicates against a series of at most eight constant values – though in practice OLAP tools that generate SQL queries often create much bigger IN clauses. A naive way to implement IN is to map it into a nested disjunctive expression;

however this tends to work well with only a handful of values. In case of many values, performance can typically be won by creating an on-the-fly hash-table, turning the predicate into a semi-join. This effect where joins turn into selections can also be viewed as a "invisible join" [13].

CP 4.2d: Evaluation Order in Conjunctions and Disjunctions. In Q19 in particular, but in multiple other queries (e.g. Q6) we see the challenge of finding the optimal evaluation order for complex boolean expressions consisting of conjunctions and disjunctions. Conjuctions can use eager evaluation, i.e. in case of (X and Y) refrain from computing expression Y if X=false. As such, an optimizer should rewrite such expressions into Y and X in case X is estimated to be less selective than Y – this problem can be generalized to arbitrarily complex boolean expressions [10]. Estimating the selectivities of the various boolean expressions may be difficult due to incomplete statistics or correlations. Also, features like range-partitioning (and partition pruning) may interact with the actually experienced selectivities – and in fact selectivities might change during query execution. For instance, in a LINEITEM table that is stored in a clustered index on l_shipdate, a range-predicate on l_receiptdate typically first experiences a selection percentage of zero, which at some point starts to rise linearly, until it reaches 100% before again linearly dropping off to zero. Therefore, there is an opportunity for dynamic, run-time schemes of determining and changing the evaluation order of boolean expressions [14]. In the case of VectorWise a 20% performance improvement was realized in Q19 by making the boolean expression operator sensitive to the observed selectivity in conjunctions, swapping left for right if the second expression is more selective regularly at run-time – and OR(x,y) being similarly optimized by rewriting it to (NOT(AND(NOT(x),NOT(y)))) followed by pushing down the inner NOTs (such that NOT($a > 2$) becomes $a \leq 2$).[3]

CP 4.3a: Rewrite LIKE(X%) into Range Query. Q2,9,13,14,16,20 contain expensive LIKE predicates; typically, string manipulations are much more costly than numerical calculations; and in Q13 it also involves l_comment, a single column that represents 33% of the entire TPC-H data volume (in VectorWise). LIKE processing has not achieved much research attention; however relying on regular expression libraries, that interpret the LIKE pattern string (assuming the pattern is a constant) is typically not very efficient. A better strategy is to have the optimizer analyze the constant pattern. A special case, is prefix search (LIKE('xxx%')) that occurs in Q14,16,20; which can be prefiltered by a less expensive string range comparison (BETWEEN 'xxx' AND 'xxy').

CP4.3b: Raw String Matching Performance. The x86 instruction set has been extended with SSE4.2 primitives that provide rather a-typical functionality: they encode 16-byte at-a-time string comparisons in a single SIMD instruction. Using such primitives can strongly speed up long string comparisons; going through 16 bytes in 4 cycles on e.g. the Nehalem core (this is 20 times faster than a normal strcmp). However, using these primitives is not always faster, as very short string comparisons that break off at the first or second byte can be better

---

[3] Swapping the evaluation should only be done if the expression is guaranteed not to trigger run-time errors nor contains NULLs – if not, query behavior could be altered.

done iteratively. Note that if string comparisons are done during group-by, as part of a hash-table lookup, they typically find an equal string and therefore have to go through it fully, such that the SSE4.2 implementation is best. In contrast, string comparisons done as part of a selection predicate might more often fall in the case where the strings are not equal, favoring the iterative approach.

CP4.3c: Regular Expression Compilation. Complex LIKE expression should best not be handled in an interpretative way, assuming that the LIKE search pattern is a constant string. The database query compiler could compile a Finite State Automaton (FSA) for recognizing the pattern. Another approach is to decompose the LIKE expression into a series of simpler functions, e.g. one that searches forward in a string and returns the new matching offset. This should be used in an iterative way, taking into account backtracking after a failed search.

2.5   CP-CorrelatedSubqueries

CP5.1: Flattening Subqueries. Many TPC-H queries have correlated subqueries. All of these query plans can be flattened, such that the correlated subquery is handled using an equi-join, outer-join or anti-join [15]. In Q21, for instance, there is an EXISTS clause (for orders with more than one supplier) and a NOT EXISTS clause (looking for an item that was received too late). To execute Q21 well, systems need to flatten both subqueries, the first into an equi-join plan, the second into an anti-join plan. Therefore, the execution layer of the database system will benefit from implementing these extended join variants.

The ill effects of repetitive tuple-at-a-time subquery execution can also be mitigated in execution systems that use vectorized, or block-wise execution, allowing to run sub-queries with thousands of input parameters instead of one. The ability to look up many keys in an index in one API call, creates the opportunity to benefit from physical locality, if lookup keys exhibit some clustering.

CP5.2: Moving Predicates into a Subquery. Q2 shows a frequent pattern: a correlated subquery which computes an aggregate that is subsequently used in a selection predicate of a similarly looking outer query ("select the minimum cost part supplier for a certain part"). Here the outer query has additional restrictions (on part type and size) that are not present in the correlated subquery, but should be propagated to it. Similar opportunities are found in Q17, and Q20.

CP5.3: Overlap between Outer- and Subquery. In Q2,11,15,17 and Q20 the correlated subquery and the outer query have the same joins and selections. In this case, a non-tree, rather DAG-shaped query plan [16] would allow to execute the common parts just once, providing the intermediate result stream to both the outer query and correlated subquery, which higher up in the query plan are joined together (using normal query decorrelation rewrites). As such, TPC-H rewards systems where the optimizer can detect this and where the execution engine sports an operator that can buffer intermediate results and provide them to multiple parent operators. In Q17, decorrelation, selective join push-down, and re-use together result in a speedup of a factor 500 in HyPer.

2.6 Parallelism and Concurrency

The TPC-H workload consists of two tests: the Power test and the Throughput test. The full query set of the former consists of the 22 TPC-H queries plus two *refresh queries*, which contain both inserts and deletes to the ORDERS and LINEITEM tables, that delete scattered ranges of orders from the orderkey space. In the Throughput test, a number of concurrent Power *query streams*, with different selection parameters, are posed to the system. The implementer can decide in the Throughput run whether to run the refresh streams in parallel with the query streams or not. For the Power test, the geometric mean of all queries results in a Power score. Using the geometric mean implies that the relative improvements to the performance of any query counts equally in the score, regardless whether this is a long-running or short-running query. The upside of this is, is that even as hardware evolves and potentially favors the performance of one query over the other, it remains interesting to optimize the full workload. On the flip-side, one can maintain that for end-users it would normally be more relevant if the long-running queries get optimized. This aspect, absolute run-time, does form part of TPC-H in the form of the Throughput score, which is derived from the full time span it takes to finish all the streams.

CP6.1: Query Plan Parallelization. When TPC-D was conceived, high-end servers would be equipped with a handful of single-core CPU chips (SMP), but very often servers would sport just a single CPU. By 2013, even single-server systems can contain 64 cores; and as such the importance of parallel query performance has increased. In the first decade of TPC-H this only affected the Power test, since it runs every query sequentially, hence it is important that the work gets divided over all cores. With only a few cores available, the Throughput test, which runs 5 (100GB) or 7 (1TB) or more query sets concurrently, could simply run sequential plans on every core and still achieve good system utilization. In the past years, however, having well-performing paralellism is important both in the Power and Throughput tests.

Query plan parallelization in the multi-core area is currently an open issue. At the time of this writing, there is active academic debate on how to parallelize the join operator on many-core architectures, with multiple sophisticated algorithms being devised and tested [17]. We can assume that the current generation of industrial systems runs less-sophisticated algorithms, and presumably in the current state may not scale linearly on many-core architectures. As such, many-core query parallelization, both in terms of query optimization and query execution is an unresolved choke point.

Further, MPP database systems from the very start focused on scaling out; typically relying on table partitioning over multiple nodes in a cluster. Table partitioning is specifically useful here in order to achieve data locality; such that queries executing in the cluster find much of the data being operated on on the local node already, without need for communication. Even in the presence of high-throughput (e.g. Infiniband) network hardware, communication bandwidth can easily become a bottleneck. For CP6, we acknowledge that the query impact color-classification in Table 1 is debatable. This classification assumes co-partitioning of ORDERS and LINEITEM to classify queries using these as medium hard or hard (if other tables are involved as well). Single-table queries parallelize trivially and are white. The idea is that with table partitioning, good parallel speedup is achievable, whereas without it this is harder. Typically, single-server multi-core parallelism does not rely on table partitioning, though it could.

CP6.2: Workload Management. Another important aspect in handling the Throughput test is workload management, which concerns providing multiple concurrent queries as they arrive, and while they run, with computational resources (RAM, cores, I/O bandwidth). The problem here is that the database system has no advance knowledge of the workload to come, hence it must adapt on-the-fly. Decisions that might seem optimal at the time of arrival of a query, might lead to avoidable thrashing if suddenly additional resource-intensive queries arrive. In the case of the Power test, workload management is trivial: it is relatively easy to devise an algorithm that while observing that maximally one query is active, assigns all resources to it. For the Throughput run, as more queries arrive, progressively less resources have to be given to the queries, until the point where there are that many queries in the system and each query gets only a single core. Since paralellism never achieves perfect scalability, in such cases of high load overall, the highest throughput tends to be achieved by running sequential plans in parallel. Workload management is even more complicated in MPP systems, since a decision needs to be made on (i) which nodes to involve in each query and (ii) how many resources per node to use.

CP6.3: Result Re-use. A final observation on the Throughput test is that with a high number of streams, i.e. beyond 20, a significant amount of identical queries emerge in the resulting workload. The reason is that certain parameters, as generated by the TPC-H workload generator, have only a limited amount of parameters bindings (e.g. there are at most 5 different values for region name r_name). This weakness opens up the possibility of using a *query result cache*, to eliminate the repetitive part of the workload. A further opportunity that detects even more overlap is the work on recycling [18], which does not only cache final query results, but also intermediate query results of "high worth". Here, worth is a combination of partial-query result size, partial-query evaluation cost, and observed (or estimated) frequency of the partial-query in the workload. It is understood in the rules of TPC-H, though, that any form of result caching should not depend on explicit DBMS configuration parameters, but reflect the default behavior of the system, in order to be admissible. This rule precludes designing re-use strategies that particularly target TPC-H, rather, such strategies should benefit most of the workloads for which the system was designed.

3   Conclusion

In this paper we have (shortly) introduced the concept of "choke points" as being the (hidden) challenges that underlie a benchmark design with the potential to stimulate technological progress. These choke points should point into relevant directions where technological advances are needed; the idea being that the benchmark gives DBMS designers a tangible reward in pursuing solutions for these. The focus of the paper, has been in applying a "post-mortem" analysis in this regard on TPC-H. We have shown that TPC-H contains a rich set of such choke points, many of which have led to advances in the state-of-the-art in analytical relational database products in the past two decades; and in fact still contains a number of unsolved challenges. Even despite its age, and arguably reduced value today, we thus argue that TPC-H as introduced in the 1990s (as TPC-D) should be an example for future benchmark designers.

References

1. Huppler, K.: The art of building a good benchmark. In: Nambiar, R., Poess, M. (eds.) TPCTC 2009. LNCS, vol. 5895, pp. 18–30. Springer, Heidelberg (2009)
2. Nambiar, R.O., Poess, M.: The making of TPC-DS. In: VLDB, pp. 1049–1058 (2006)
3. Simmen, D.E., Shekita, E.J., Malkemus, T.: Fundamental techniques for order optimization. In: Jagadish, H.V., Mumick, I.S. (eds.) Proceedings of the 1996 ACM SIGMOD International Conference on Management of Data, Montreal, Quebec, Canada, June 4-6, pp. 57–67. ACM Press (1996)
4. Moerkotte, G., Neumann, T.: Accelerating queries with group-by and join by groupjoin. PVLDB 4, 843–851 (2011)
5. Graefe, G.: Query evaluation techniques for large databases. ACM Comput. Surv. 25, 73–170 (1993)
6. Neumann, T., Weikum, G.: Scalable join processing on very large rdf graphs. In: Proceedings of the 35th SIGMOD International Conference on Management of Data, pp. 627–640. ACM (2009)
7. Rao, J., Lindsay, B., Lohman, G., Pirahesh, H., Simmen, D.: Using EELs: A practical approach to outerjoin and antijoin reordering. In: ICDE, pp. 595–606 (2001)
8. Moerkotte, G., Neumann, T.: Dynamic programming strikes back. In: SIGMOD Conference, pp. 539–552 (2008)
9. Ilyas, I.F., Markl, V., Haas, P.J., Brown, P., Aboulnaga, A.: Cords: Automatic discovery of correlations and soft functional dependencies. In: SIGMOD Conference, pp. 647–658 (2004)
10. Moerkotte, G.: Small materialized aggregates: A light weight index structure for data warehousing. In: VLDB, pp. 476–487 (1998)
11. Zukowski, M., Nes, N., Boncz, P.A.: DSM vs. NSM: Cpu performance tradeoffs in block-oriented query processing. In: DaMoN, pp. 47–54 (2008)
12. Abadi, D.J.: Query execution in column-oriented database systems. MIT PhD Dissertation (2008) PhD Thesis
13. Abadi, D.J., Madden, S., Hachem, N.: Column-stores vs. row-stores: how different are they really? In: SIGMOD Conference, pp. 967–980 (2008)
14. Li, Q., Shao, M., Markl, V., Beyer, K.S., Colby, L.S., Lohman, G.M.: Adaptively reordering joins during query execution. In: ICDE, pp. 26–35 (2007)
15. Seshadri, P., Pirahesh, H., Leung, T.Y.C.: Complex query decorrelation. In: ICDE, pp. 450–458 (1996)
16. Neumann, T., Moerkotte, G.: A framework for reasoning about share equivalence and its integration into a plan generator. In: BTW, pp. 7–26 (2009)
17. Balkesen, C., Teubner, J., Alonso, G., Özsu, M.T.: Main-memory hash joins on multi-core cpus: Tuning to the underlying hardware. In: ICDE (2013)
18. Nagel, F., Boncz, P., Viglas, S.D.: Recycling in pipelined query evaluation. In: ICDE (2013)

Architecture and Performance Characteristics of a PostgreSQL Implementation of the TPC-E and TPC-V Workloads

Andrew Bond[1], Douglas Johnson[2], Greg Kopczynski[3], and H. Reza Taheri[3]

[1] Red Hat, Inc.
[2] InfoSizing, Inc.
[3] VMware, Inc.
abond@redhat.com, doug@sizing.com, {gregwk,rtaheri}@vmware.com

Abstract. The TPC has been developing a publicly available, end-to-end benchmarking kit to run the new TPC-V benchmark, with the goal of measuring the performance of databases subjected to the variability and elasticity of load demands that are common in cloud environments. This kit is being developed completely from scratch in Java and C++ with PostgreSQL as the target database. Since the TPC-V workload is based on the mature TPC-E benchmark, the kit initially implements the TPC-E schema and transactions. In this paper, we will report on the status of the kit, describe the architectural details, and provide results from prototyping experiments at performance levels that are representative of enterprise-class databases. We are not aware of other PostgreSQL benchmarking results running at the levels we will describe in the paper. We will list the optimizations that were made to PostgreSQL parameters, to hardware/operating system/file system settings, and to the benchmarking code to maximize the performance of PostgreSQL, and saturate a large, 4-socket server.

Keywords: Database performance, virtualization, PostgreSQL, cloud computing.

1 Introduction

1.1 TPC-V Benchmark

In this paper, we will describe the architecture of the TPC-V benchmark, give a progress report on its implementation, and present the performance results collected so far. TPC-V measures the performance of a server running virtualized databases. It is similar to previous virtualization benchmarks in that it has many VMs running different workloads. It is also similar to previous TPC benchmarks in that it uses the schema and transactions of the TPC-E benchmark. But TPC-V is unique since unlike previous virtualization benchmarks, it has a database-centric workload, and models many properties of cloud servers, such as multiple VMs running at different load demand levels, and large fluctuations in the load level of each VM. Unlike previous TPC benchmarks, TPC-V will have a publicly-available, end-to-end benchmarking kit.

R. Nambiar and M. Poess (Eds.): TPCTC 2013, LNCS 8391, pp. 77–92, 2014.

We will start with a short introduction to virtualization, give a brief background on the properties and the development process of the benchmark, then describe the architecture of the kit, and conclude with some of the performance results obtained so far.

1.2   Virtualization

Virtualization on the Intel x86 architecture was pioneered in late 1990s [2, 3, 4], and has grown to become a mainstream technology used in enterprise datacenters. Today, virtualization is the fundamental technology that enables cloud computing. So, there is strong demand for a database-centric virtualization performance benchmark with cloud computing characteristics. In response to this demand, a TPC subcommittee was formed in 2010 to develop a benchmark with the following properties:

1. Models a database-centric workload
2. Exercises the virtualization layer
3. Has a moderate number of VMs (as opposed to modeling a pure consolidation scenario with a large number of VMs)
4. Emulates a mix of Transaction Processing and Decision Support workloads
5. A heterogeneous mix of low load volume and high load volume VMs
6. Has a healthy storage and networking I/O content
7. Models the elastic load-level variations of cloud VMs

The complete description of the benchmark specification, the details of the load variation, performance metrics, and other properties of the benchmark are detailed in [1, 5]. In this paper, we will describe the new developments and prototyping results.

2   Other Virtualization Benchmarks

2.1   Consolidation Benchmarks

The early virtualization benchmarks were representative of the consolidation environment where many low volume workloads that had been running on individual servers would be consolidated onto a single server using virtualization. The earliest example is VMmark [14] which is a de facto standard with hundreds of publication on several succeeding versions of the benchmark. An industry standard follow-on is SPECvirt_sc2010 [7] which incorporates modified versions of three SPEC workloads (SPECweb2005_Support, SPECjAppServer2004 and SPECmail2008) and drives them simultaneously to emulate virtualized server consolidation environments, much like VMmark 1.0 did. To date, there have been 33 publications on SPECvirt_sc2010. The SPECvirt_sc2013 [9] benchmark was released in 2013 with 2 publications so far.

2.2   TPC-VMS

In 2012, the TPC released the TPC-VMS [7] (TPC Virtual Measurement Single System) benchmark, which emulates a simple consolidation scenario of 3 identical databases. The 4 workloads used in TPC-VMS are the TPC-C [10], TPC-E [11], TPC-H [12], and TPC-DS [13] benchmarks. By leveraging existing TPC benchmarks,

TPC-VMS does not require development of a new kit. It is expected that the ease of benchmarking afforded by use of existing kits will result in vendors publishing TPC-VMS results while the more feature-rich TPC-V benchmark is being developed.

3 TPC-V Architecture

3.1 TPC-E as a Starting Point

We decided early on to base the TPC-V workload on the existing TPC-E [11] benchmark. The *long pole* in benchmark development is often the development of the schema and the transactions, as well as writing a crisp, detailed specification that lays out the detailed documentation required for audit and publication procedures. By borrowing the Data Definition Language (DDL) and Data Manipulation Language (DML) of TPC-E, we were able to start the prototyping of TPC-V much earlier than is typical of TPC benchmarks. And by using the TPC-E functional specification document as the starting point, we only had to focus on what is new in TPC-V. TPC-V is fundamentally a different benchmark from TPC-E with different characteristics, yet gained years of development time by using TPC-E as the foundation.

3.1.1 Differences with TPC-E
Like TPC-E, TPC-V has 33 tables and 12 transactions, and very similar DDL and DML. However, there are differences in table cardinalities and the transaction mix, mostly to make the benchmarks non-comparable and for ease of benchmarking [1].

3.1.2 VGen
EGen, a publicly available program, generates the raw data that is used to populate a TPC-E database. It is also linked with the benchmarking kit to produce the run time transaction parameters. This ensures that query arguments match what has been loaded into the database. It also governs the generation of many run-time parameters, such as the transaction mix frequencies and random numbers. Besides making it easier to develop benchmarking kits, this guarantees adherence to the benchmark specification

TPC-V follows this model by using a VGen module that is based on EGen, modified to conform to the TPC-V specification. As will be detailed in section 3, the TPC-V benchmarking kit must produce different volumes of load to different VMs (section 3.2), and vary this load at different phases of the benchmark run (section 3.4). We realized early on that driving the load to different VMs independently and attempting to keep them in sync at run time would be nearly impossible. Instead, all of these relationships are maintained by VGen. It distributes transactions over VMs following the numerical quantities specified in a configuration file, and also varies the load based on the elasticity parameters in that file. Using a deck of cards method, VGen ensures that the load ratios among the many VMs are maintained at the values specified in the configuration file. If one VM is running slower than expected, the load to other VMs is automatically reduced such that the specified ratios are maintained.

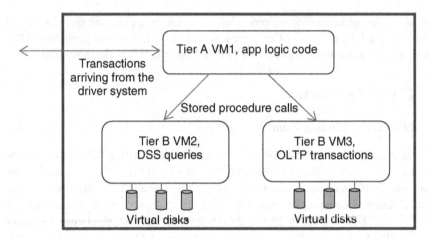

Fig. 1. Components of a TPC-V **Set**

3.2   Heterogeneous Load

The basic building block of TPC-V is a Set of 3 VMs. Tier A VM1 receives transactions from the driver system and runs the database client code, similar to the Tier A of a TPC-E benchmark configuration [11]. VM1 directs the two Decision Support transactions to the DSS VM2, and the other transactions to the OLTP VM3. Each VM has an independent database instance that resides on that VM's virtual disk drives.

3.3   Multiple Sets and Groups

Fig. 2 represents the simplest TPC-V configuration of a server with 4 Groups, each with one Set of 3 VMs for a total of 12 VMs. To emulate the heterogeneous nature of VMs in a cloud environment, each Group handles a different proportion of the overall load. Averaged over the full measurement interval, Groups A, B, C, and   D   receive 10%, 20%, 30%, and 40% of the overall load, respectively. The sizes of the independent databases in the 4 VMs (represented by table cardinalities) follow the same proportions. The 4 Groups are driven independently; the driver module is required to ensure that the load proportions remain as specified.

Group A, Set 1	VM1 A1	VM2	VM3 A1
Group B, Set 1	VM1 B1	VM2 B1	VM3 B1
Group C, Set 1	VM1 C1	VM2 C1	VM3 C1
Group D, Set 1	VM1 D1	VM2 D1	VM3 D1

Fig. 2. A TPC-V server with 4 Groups and 12 VMs

The number of Sets per Group in TPC-V grows as the overall throughput grows. So, e.g., at a throughput level of 4,000 tpsV, the sponsor is required to configure 2 Sets per Group. For Group A, each of the two Sets supplies 5% of the overall throughput; a similar calculus applies to the other three Groups. The growth in the number of Sets per Group is sub-linear: a 10X throughput growth might result in a 2X increase in the number of Sets per Group. This is characteristic of database servers in the cloud.

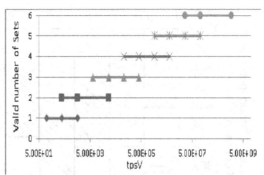

Fig. 3. Overlapping ranges for valid numbers of Sets per Group

Rather than requiring an exact number of Sets for every throughput value, we allow two possible Set counts for most throughput ranges, as shown in Table 1 and Fig. 3. This was done for ease of benchmarking. Without this allowance, if a test sponsor were targeting a throughput that is near the value at which the number of Sets per Group changes, a slight change up or down in the eventual throughput would necessitate rebuilding the testing infrastructure with a different number of VMs.

Table 1. Valid numbers of Sets for various throughputs

From tpsV	To tpsV	No. of Sets
100	1600	1
400	25,600	2
6,300	409,500	3
102,400	6,553,600	4
1,638,400	104,857,600	5
26,214,000	Infinity	6

So, for example, 25,600 tpsV is the crossing point from 2 to 3 Sets per group. If the sponsor expects to achieve 25,600 tpsV, builds a 3-Sets-per-Group configuration with 36 VMs and 24 databases, but reaches only 24,000 tpsV, there is no need to reconfigure platform with fewer VMs since the specification allows 3 Sets per Group down to 6,300 tpsV. The sponsor only needs to repopulate the databases, scaled to the correct throughput.

3.4   Elasticity

A feature of TPC-V is that the load of each Set rises and falls during the measurement interval. This represents the elastic nature of workloads present in cloud data centers, and the resource allocation policies required to handle such elasticity. The overall load presented to the System Under Test remains constant during the Measurement Interval, but the contribution from each Set varies by as much as a factor of 7X every 12 minutes, e.g., the rise of the contribution of Group A from 5% to 35% in Elasticity

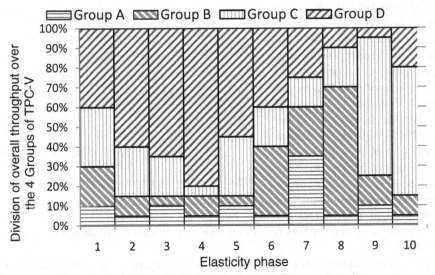

Fig. 4. Distribution of overall load over the 4 Groups versus time

Table 2. Phase-to-phase variation of load received by individual Groups

Elasticity Phase	Group A	Group B	Group C	Group D
1	10%	20%	30%	40%
2	5%	10%	25%	60%
3	10%	5%	20%	65%
4	5%	10%	5%	80%
5	10%	5%	30%	55%
6	5%	35%	20%	40%
7	35%	25%	15%	25%
8	5%	65%	20%	10%
9	10%	15%	70%	5%
10	5%	10%	65%	20%
Average	10%	20%	30%	40%

Phase 7. When the contribution of a Group changes, the contribution of all individual Sets in that Group change to the same degree. Table 2 and Fig. 4 show how much each Set contributes to the overall throughput in each 12-minute Elasticity Phase.

4   Reference Kit

Benchmarking kits for TPC benchmarks have always been provided by test sponsors, typically by DBMS vendors who tailor their kits to their own databases. Although we would have liked a DBMS vendor to provide a benchmarking kit for TPC-V, due to lack of such a commitment, the subcommittee accepted the challenge of developing its own kit. This turned out to be a positive development as it will result in the TPC releasing its first publicly available, complete end-to-end benchmarking kit which can be used by system vendors, researchers, and end users alike. The details of this decision making, comparison with other benchmarking kits, and a block diagram of the kit components can be found in [1]. Fig. 5 shows how the various elements of the TPC-V reference kit map to the components of the tested configurations.

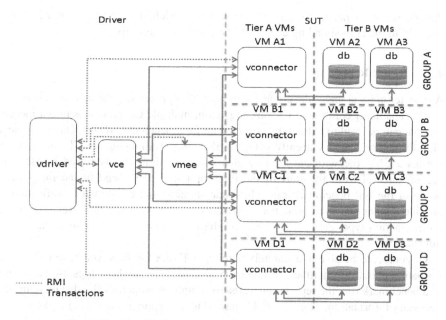

Fig. 5. Single-set Reference Driver Components Representation

4.1 V-Gen Functionality Development

The primary focus in implementing V-Gen functionality has been in adding multi-group, multi-set, multi-phase support. And while multi-group and multi-set and multi-phase have been described previously, the multi-iteration support has been added in order to be able to run as many ten-phase intervals as desired in a single test. The tester will then be able to choose any sequential ten phases in the multi-interval test run as the measurement set. The ability to choose such a measurement set is being added to a reporter process, which is also new to the kit. And lastly, the runtime result polling has been modified to provide group mix data that displays performance on a per-group basis in addition to the previous per-transaction basis.

4.2 Card Deck for Multi-group, Multi-set and Multi-phase Support

As described previously, multi-group and multi-set support has been implemented in the reference driver by having every CE process connect to each vconnector process in every group and every set. In doing so, we are able to use a card deck to assure the proper mix of transactions across these groups and sets. This deck is created for each CE load generating thread and is shuffled at the beginning of the run. Each time the CE starts a new request, it takes a card from this deck to determine the group and set ID of the vconnector process to whom it should direct the request, and once the bottom of the deck is reached, it simply starts back at the top.

Likewise, different phases have different transaction mixes, so we have a separate card deck for each of the ten phases that contains the proper mix of transactions for that phase. At a phase change, the deck from which the cards are pulled is also changed to the corresponding deck with the correct request mix.

4.3   Result Reporting

A reporter class is under development to help with processing the mix logs. It is currently capable of combining CE mix logs from multiple CE processes into a merged log that can be used to extract the needed data for a benchmark report. One such piece of information that it currently offers is that after combining the CE mix logs, it creates a CSV file with the total number of transactions that occurred in each 30-second interval from the start of the ramp-up-phase to the end of the ramp-down phase of the full benchmark run. This code should require minimal modification to provide similar and more granular information on transaction totals over time based on transaction type, group, set, iteration, phase, or even per-client-thread transaction information.

Of course, to be able to accurately combine CE mix log files, you have to have information about the runtime configuration used to generate those logs. So at the end of a benchmark run, the reporter also creates a runtime.properties file that contains the necessary information. This file is also passed to the reporter when it is invoked.

4.4   Runtime Polling

The addition of groups and sets to TPC-V resulted in the need for group- and set-specific polling information. So in addition to the previous per-transaction-type

```
----------------------------------------------------------------------
                     Txn Rate   Resp Time   Txn Pct   Pass Count   Fail Count
TRADE_ORDER       :     8.36      0.0077      11.33       1487          18
TRADE_RESULT      :     0.00           0       0.00          0           0
TRADE_LOOKUP      :     6.60      0.4995       8.95       1188           0
TRADE_UPDATE      :     1.66      0.6165       2.25        299           0
TRADE_STATUS      :    15.94      0.0074      21.60       2869           0
CUSTOMER_POSITION :    10.67      0.0076      14.46       1920           0
BROKER_VOLUME     :     4.09      0.0402       5.54        736           0
SECURITY_DETAIL   :    11.68      0.0067      15.83       2102           0
MARKET_FEED       :     0.00           0       0.00          0           0
MARKET_WATCH      :    14.78      0.0104      20.04       2661           0
DATA_MAINTENANCE  :     0.00           0       0.00          0           0
TRADE_CLEANUP     :     0.00           0       0.00          0           0
----------------------------------------------------------------------


-----------------------------------------------------------------
               Group 1     Group 2     Group 3     Group 4
Txn Total:        664        1329        3316        7971
Txn Pct  :       5.00       10.01       24.97       60.02
Resp Time:     0.0957      0.0771      0.0705      0.0624
Fail Cnt :          2           2           3          11
-----------------------------------------------------------------

Iteration 2 Phase 2 Aggregate Txn Rate: 73.78
```

Fig. 6. Sample polling output

polling information, per-group polling information has been added. So now a sample polling output might look like the output in Fig. 6. This additional information lets you know whether you are meeting the transaction mix requirements for each group, as well as the average response times and failure counts for each vconnector process.

4.5   MEE Development

As already noted, the MEE currently implements the Market Feed and Trade Result transactions as required for TPC-E. However, the nature of the MEE is such that it places constraints on implementation design for TPC-V. For example, we cannot design the MEE such that a single MEE process connects to all groups and sets as we do with the CE. This is because when transactions from the CE that trigger MEE transactions occur, they do not identify themselves by their group and set. Thus when the MEE generates a transaction in response to the CE trigger, it would have no way of knowing which vconnector process should be the recipient of this transaction.

Due to this design constraint, we need a MEE paired specifically with each vconnector process so that any CE request that triggers and MEE transaction will always be sent to the correct recipient. At this point, this could mean a separate MEE process is started for each vconnector process, but ideally we hope to be able to have one MEE process handle requests for all four groups in each set using separate transaction handling threads and requiring only unique connections for each of these four MEE threads. This is not a requirement, though having fewer processes for the prime client to coordinate with is certainly desirable.

4.6   TPC-E Functionality

Since TPC-E is the starting point of this benchmark, and since it is a simpler, single-system benchmark, we used it as the design center of the first implementation of the reference kit. Although a complete, compliant TPC-E kit is not a goal of this project, the early prototype has been used to provide a glimpse of PostgreSQL running the TPC-E workload. Although we have been experimenting with multiple Sets and VMs following the TPC-V architecture, the workload has been mostly based on TPC-E.

5   Current Status of the Benchmark and the Reference Kit

The TPC-V reference benchmarking kit is nearly complete as of this writing. Below are the functionalities that are completed:

- A Driver module that generates TPC-E or TPC-V transactions, and distributes them over any number of Set and Groups of VMs in case of TPC-V (see section 3). It also implements the TPC-V elasticity feature
- A VGen module based on the TPC-V schema, transaction mix, etc.
- The Customer Emulator module
- The Market Exchange Emulator module for TPC-E transactions
- The vconnector module that performs all the database accesses

- The DDL and DML scripts for PostgreSQL 9.2
- Linux shell scripts to launch all these programs, collect data and statistics, and produce results metrics

The functionalities that remain to be completed are:

- Modifying the MEE, stored procedures, and DML calls such that the Trade-Result and Market-Feed transactions conform to the TPC-V specification
- The Data-maintenance transaction (a non-critical component)
- Extensive prototyping results for verification and testing of the reference kit
- Porting of the reference kit to multiple environments

6   Results from Prototyping Experiments

6.1   Introduction

Most of the results presented here were obtained before the MEE functionality was added to the kit. So they are not an accurate representation of eventual TPC-V performance. However, we expect the two missing transactions to have similar profiles to the 8 transactions implemented. The current functionality is sufficient to study how efficiently PostgreSQL executes the TPC-E/TPC-V queries, as well as an analysis of whether the hypervisor used in the study was able to handle the variability and elasticity of the load that TPC-V places on the system. For the remainder of this section, we will refer to transactions per second or tps to denote the total number of transactions processed. This should not be confused with the tpsV metric, which only counts the Trade-Result transactions, which make up only a 10% fraction of the total transaction volume. Trade-Result is issued by the MEE module, which was not developed in time for our initial measurements. Hence we count all 8 transactions, and report that as tps.

6.2   Benchmarking Configuration

The system under test was a 4-socket HP ProLiant DL580 G7 server with 2.40GHz Intel Xeon E7-4870 (WestmereEX) CPUs. To put this in perspective, HP has published a TPC-E result of 2,454 tpsE[1] on this system. The highest TPC-E result is 5,457 tpsE on an IBM System X3850 X5 server[2]. So the server we are using for prototyping is a large, high-end server. The storage was two EMC VNX5700 disk arrays. 38 EFDs (EMC term for SSDs) in a RAID5 configurations were used for the DSS VMs, which have the lion's share of disk I/O. 88 spinning disk drives in a RAID 1 configuration were used for the OLTP VMs, which have lower I/O requirements. The software stack was vSphere 5.1, RHEL 6.1, PostgreSQL 9.2.2 and unixODBC 2.2.14.

The benchmark was configured with 1 Set for each of the 4 Groups, for a total of 12 VMs. The driver system was the 13th VMs on the system. The database size is expressed in Load Units, each LU representing 1,000 rows in the Customers table. The cardinalities of the other 32 tables are either fixed, or are proportional to the number of Customers.

---

[1] As of 6/21/2013. Complete details available at http://www.tpc.org/4046
[2] As of 6/21/2013. Complete details available at http://www.tpc.org/4063

Table 3. Configuration info for VMs

	VM A1	VM A2	VM A3	VM B1	VM B2	VM B3	VM C1	VM C2	VM C3	VM D1	VM D2	VM D3
DB size in LUs	-	50	50	-	100	100	-	150	150	-	200	200
DB size in GB	-	336	328	-	670	654	-	1004	980	-	1308	1328
Memory in GB	2	88	39	2	146	54	2	220	68	2	278	78
vCPUs	3	4	12	5	8	24	6	12	30	8	16	40

Table 3 shows various configuration parameters for the 12 VMs. VM1s have very little memory usage, and their CPU usage is about $1/8^{th}$ of the total CPU load. VM2s have modest processing needs, but we had to allocate most of the memory to them to cache more of the database and reduce the I/O load. VM3s didn't need as much memory since their I/O was already low, but were allocated about 60% of the total processing power. It is worth noting that, much like real cloud database VMs, although the CPU resources were *overcommitted* (more virtual CPUs in the VMs than physical CPUs on the server), the total memory allocated to the 12 VMs is 979GB, on a server with 1TB of memory. This is common for database VMs since overcommitting memory can result in paging, with disastrous results for database performance.

Virtual CPUs and Elasticity

The number of virtual CPUs, however, totals 168, well above the 80 logical CPUs (40 cores X 2 hyperthreads per core) on the server. This overcommitting is common in cloud environments since the number of virtual CPUs configured into a VM should be adequate for its peak demand. But not all VMs peak at the same time. So as long as the total load does not exceed 80 CPUs' worth, we can overcommit the virtual CPUs.

6.3   1-Phase and 10-Phase Runs

As mentioned in section 3.4, TPC-V requires the load received by each Group to vary over ten 12-minute elasticity phases. As we will see in section 6.4, this posed a challenge in our environment due to storage bandwidth limitations. So we ran some experiments with a single phase (i.e., constant proportioning of load across Sets for the duration of the run) to study the performance characteristics of the database, the operating, the hypervisor, and the hardware. We also ran experiments with 10 phases to specifically study the ability of the system under test to respond to load elasticity, and to determine whether the TPC-V benchmarking kit is able to deterministically distribute the load over the Sets even when some Sets are strained under the load.

In a 1-phase run with 4 Groups, the throughput was 4,191 transactions per second[3]. In the CPU utilization graphs in Fig. 7, the Y axis is the total CPU utilization of each

---

[3] As mentioned in section 6.1, this *transactions per second* metric should not be confused with the tpsV metric, which would have been as much as an order of magnitude smaller.

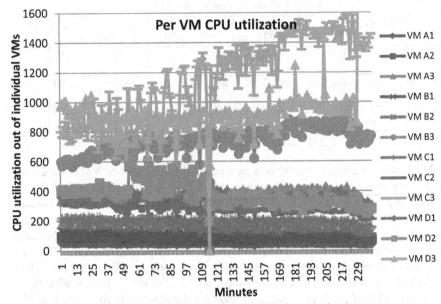

Fig. 7. CPU utilization of individual VMs for a single-phase run

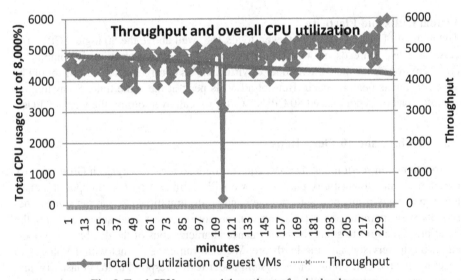

Fig. 8. Total CPU usage and throughput of a single-phase run

VM. An 8-vCPU VM would register a utilization of 800% if all 8 vCPUs were fully utilized. All of these metrics are measured on virtual CPUs on the guest VMs.

Fig. 8 shows throughput and the sum of CPU utilizations of individual VMs. It might appear that the system is not fully saturated, but that's due to the artifacts of hyperthreading when we collect statistics on the guest OS. Hypervisor and hardware counters register between 85% and 95% utilization on the CPU cores.

6.4   Throughput versus Other Performance Metrics for 10-Phase Runs

We also ran the benchmark with the load variation depicted in Fig. 4. As Fig. 9 shows, the CPU utilizations of individual VMs varied during the 2-hour runs, as did the overall throughput, shown in Fig. 10. However, the benchmarking kit ensured that the contributions of each Group remained exactly as prescribed in Table 2.

In this case, the throughput dropped drastically during some phases. The reason for this drop was the inability of the storage to cope with the changes in load. Briefly, the

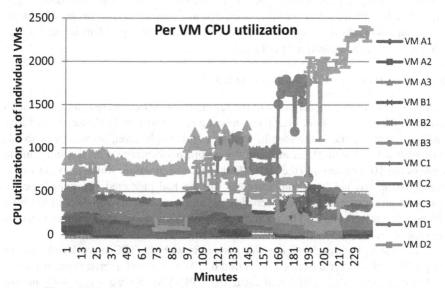

Fig. 9. CPU utilizations of individual VMs for a run with 10 elasticity phases

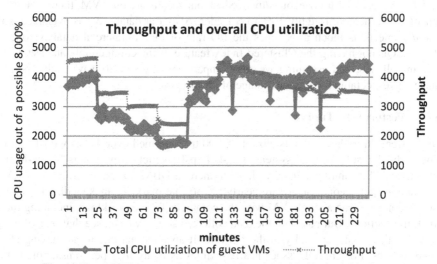

Fig. 10. Total CPU usage and throughput for a run with 10 elasticity phases

overall load, and hence the overall I/O requirements, remain constant over the execution time. Hence, if the storage is shared by all VMs in a striped format, the variations in load should not have the large impact that we observed. However, our storage was split in two groups: LUNs for Groups A and B were striped across one set of SSD disks, and LUNs for Groups C and D on a second set of SSD drives.

When in Phase 4 the load of the Group D is at its maximum, the second storage array was unable to satisfy the needs of that Group. One can overlay Fig. 4 and Fig. 10, and see that whenever Group C or Group D is at or near peak contribution to the overall throughput, performance goes down because we are unable to utilize excess capacity left in the first storage array dedicated to Groups A and B. In other words the benchmark is working exactly as intended: it is exposing a problem in the resource management of the underlying platform.

6.5   Results with a Full, End-to-End Kit

As pointed out in section 6.1, most of the results reported here were from a kit that did not have the MEE module, i.e., it was missing the important Trade-Result and Market-Feed transactions. In the months leading to this publication, we were able to take runs with a functional MEE, and could measure performance with the full complement of the 10 transactions (the Data-Maintenance transaction, which does not impact performance, has not been implemented). As we had predicted, the overall performance in terms of average milliseconds/transaction and the overall execution profile did not change very much. The addition of the two new transactions only changed the frequency percentages of the mix of transactions.

Early results look encouraging. We took runs with the TPC-E workload on a 16-way VM on the server described in section 6.2. We observed a throughput of roughly 140 tpsE at 80% CPU utilization on a 16-vCPU VM. So we are at ~9.1 milliseconds/tpsE. The published result with a commercial DBMS for this 80-way server is 2,454 tpsE, i.e. ~3.3 milliseconds/tpsE. Since our results are on a VM, there is a virtualization overhead of roughly 10% to consider. Also, our database was oversized, and our I/O rate is as much as 8 times the I/O rate of the commercial database due to PostgreSQL not having the Clustered Index feature of the commercial database. Considering all this, and assuming we can compare 16-way and 80-way results, performance is respectable for this early stage of prototyping.

6.6   PostgreSQL Tuning

Our current throughput level is close to 5,000 tps, summed over 4 Sets with 12 VMs. The audited result for this system is 2,454 tpsE, which only counts Trade-Result transactions. So running TPC-E with a commercial DBMS, it really processes 24,545 transactions per second. So we are nearly 5X off that mark. To make a direct comparison, we need to run a single VM with the complete TPC-E workload, including the 2 MEE transactions. But based on the data collected so far, we can see that many tuning opportunities exist, especially in the I/O rate. It appears that due to not having clustered indexes, PostgreSQL issues nearly 4 times as many I/Os per transaction as the TPC-E design goal. This is our primary focus area for the next phase of this project.

Table 4. I/O stats for DSS VM with one and two 2 file

		wrqm/s	r/s	w/s	rkB/s	wkB/s	avgrq	avgqu	await
1 FS	Data+log	1830	11151	2767	138602	33956	25	30	2.14
2 FS	data	2406	12350	2278	181902	18737	27	40	2.71
	log	343	0.34	134	1	17854	264	0.3	1.87

Table 5. I/O stats for OLTP VM with one and two 2 file systems

		wrqm/s	r/s	w/s	rkB/s	wkB/s	avgrq	avgqu	await
1 FS	Data+log	403	542	476	7682	5552	27	5.1	4.75
2 FS	Data	194	860	145	15613	1357	34	6.3	6.29
	log	1	0.04	225	0.16	3066	27	0.3	1.15

File System Parameters

An optimization recommend in [6] is separate file systems for data and Write-Ahead Log (WAL), because of the more strict cache flushing semantics for the log. Initially, an ext4 file system held both log and data, mounted with noatime, nodiratime, nobarrier,. We then created a pg-xlog ext3 file system, mounted with noatime, nodiratime, data=writeback. The log virtual disks of all VMs were placed on a LUN with only 4 disk drives, yet all experienced fast disk latencies. The result was a 6.5% increase in the throughput of the 4-Group, single-phase runs to 4,769 tps.

Checkpointing

Two parameters manage the checkpoint frequency of PostgreSQL. A new checkpoint is initiated either when a checkpoint has not occurred in checkpoint_timeout minutes, or when checkpoint_segments 16MB WAL segments have been used since the last checkpoint. We increased checkpoint_timeout from the default of 3 minutes to 30, and checkpoint_segments from the default of 3 to 128, believing 128 checkpoint_segments were enough, even for the largest VM, to let checkpointing be governed by checkpoint_timeout. Tests, however, showed that we were checkpointing as often as once every 2 minutes. We needed to increase checkpoint_segments to 1,920 segments on the largest VM; we used 5,120 to be safe. This change gave us a 2% improvement to 4,841 tps. Table 6 has the *background writer stats* section of the pgstatspack outputs before and after the change for 30-minute runs. The checkpoints_timed and checkpoints_req counts show that originally, there were 15 checkpoints triggered because the database had used all the WAL segments, and none due to reaching the checkpoint frequency timer. After increasing the number of WAL segments, we see only a single time-triggered checkpoint.

Table 6. Effects of increasing WAL_segments

Checkpoint metric	12 segments	5,120 segments
checkpoints_timed	0	1
checkpoints_req	15	0
buffers_checkpoint	4,437,177	956,174
buffers_clean	14,069	852,893
buffers_backend	46,297	39,297
buffers_alloc	24,831,473	23,749,499

7   Conclusions

The TPC-V reference benchmarking kit, which is at the heart of the benchmark, is nearly complete. It provides all the novel properties of TPC-V: a heterogeneous combination of workloads driven to many VMs, a deterministic distribution of load over the VMs regardless of how each VM handles the load, and dynamically varying the load levels to VMs to emulate the elasticity of load in the cloud. Using this kit, we have discovered several optimizations for a PostgreSQL implementation of TPC-V.

Acknowledgements. We thank Cecil Reames for VGen and specification reviews, Matt Emmerton, John Fowler, and Jamie Reding for TPC-E knowledge, Karl Huppler and Wayne Smith for high level benchmark requirements, and Jignesh Shah for PostgreSQL advice.

References

1. Bond, A., Kopczynski, G., Reza Taheri, H.: Two Firsts for the TPC: A Benchmark to Characterize Databases Virtualized in the Cloud, and a Publicly-Available, Complete End-to-End Reference Kit. In: Nambiar, R., Poess, M. (eds.) TPCTC 2012. LNCS, vol. 7755, pp. 34–50. Springer, Heidelberg (2013)
2. Figueiredo, R., Dinda, P.A., Fortes, J.A.B.: 'Guest Editors' Introduction: Resource Virtualization Renaissance. Computer 38(5), 28–31 (2005), http://www2.computer.org/portal/web/csdl/doi/10.1109/MC.2005.159
3. Nanda, S., Chiueh, T.-C.: A Survey on Virtualization Technologies. Technical Report ECSL-TR-179, SUNY at Stony Brook (February 2005), http://www.ecsl.cs.sunysb.edu/tr/TR179.pdf
4. Rosenblum, M., Garfinkel, T.: Virtual Machine Monitors: Current Technology and Future Trends. Computer 38(5), 39–47 (2005)
5. Sethuraman, P., Reza Taheri, H.: TPC-V: A Benchmark for Evaluating the Performance of Database Applications in Virtual Environments. In: Nambiar, R., Poess, M. (eds.) TPCTC 2010. LNCS, vol. 6417, pp. 121–135. Springer, Heidelberg (2011)
6. Smith, G.: PostgreSQL 9.0 High Performance. Packt Publishing (October 20, 2010)
7. Smith, W.D., Sebastian, S.: Virtualization Performance Insights from TPC-VMS, http://www.tpc.org/tpcvms/tpc-vms-2013-1.0.pdf
8. SPECvirt_sc2010 benchmark info, SPEC Virtualization Committee, http://www.spec.org/virt_sc2010/
9. SPECvirt_sc2013 benchmark info, SPEC Virtualization Committee, http://www.spec.org/virt_sc2013/
10. TPC: Detailed TPC-C description, http://www.tpc.org/tpcc/detail.asp
11. TPC: Detailed TPC-E Description, http://www.tpc.org/tpce/spec/TPCEDetailed.doc
12. TPC: TPC Benchmark H Specification, http://www.tpc.org/tpch/spec/tpch2.14.4.pdf
13. TPC: TPC Benchmark DS Specification, http://www.tpc.org/tpcds/spec/tpcds_1.1.0.pdf
14. VMware, Inc., http://www.vmware.com/products/vmmark/overview.html

A Practice of TPC-DS Multidimensional Implementation on NoSQL Database Systems

Hongwei Zhao and Xiaojun Ye

School of Software, Tsinghua University, Beijing 100084, China
hwzhao73@gmail.com, yexj@tsinghua.edu.cn

Abstract. While NoSQL database systems are well established, it is not clear how to process multidimensional OLAP queries on current key-value stores. In this paper, we detail how to match the high-level cube model with the low-level key-value stores built on NoSQL databases, and illustrate how to support efficiently OLAP queries by scale out while retaining a MapReduce-like execution engine. For big data the functional problem of storage and processing power is compounded, we balanced them with partial aggregation between batch processing and query runtime. Base cuboids are initially constructed for TPC-DS fact tables by using multidimensional array, and cuboids for various granularity aggregation data are derived at runtime with base ones. The cube storage module converts dimension members into binary keys and leverages a novel distributed database to provide efficient storage for huge cuboids. The OLAP engine built on lightweight concurrent actors can scale out seamlessly; provide highly concurrent distributed cuboid processing. Finally, we illustrate some experiments on the implementation prototype based on TPC-DS queries. The results show that multidimensional models for OLAP applications on NoSQL systems are possible for future big data analytics.

Keywords: Big Data, On Line Analysis Processing, Multidimensional Data Model, TPC-DS Benchmark.

1   Motivation

Scalability and flexibility create challenges on earlier-generation Business Intelligence (BI) technologies and infrastructure architectures [1]. On Line Analysis Processing (OLAP) engine, one of BI components, faces a confluence of growing challenges deriving from the latest big data revolution [2]. Although business analytics over large-scale data repositories have been investigated recently, such as Dremel [3], Spanner [4] and Spark [5], the problem of integrating multidimensional data models on top of distributed file systems and extending typical OLAP operators in the context of big data analytics are not clear in current NoSQL database systems.

Purposes of OLAP engines are to provide roll-up/drill-down, slice/dice or pivot capabilities on data warehouse systems. But the limitations in MOLAP are that it is not very scalable and can only handle limited amounts of data since calculations are predefined (storage and cache) in the cube. OLAP engines have to take an

R. Nambiar and M. Poess (Eds.): TPCTC 2013, LNCS 8391, pp. 93–108, 2014.
© Springer International Publishing Switzerland 2014

evolutionary architecture that is going to employ distribution and parallel computing technologies. In this paper, we propose a distributed OLAP server implementation approach with cube model in order to fill the gap between big data stores and rapid interactive business analytic demands. Compared to traditional OLAP servers, it's easily scaled out for big data analytic and kept low latency by paralleling query processing tasks with fault tolerance provided by underlying NoSQL database systems.

1.1 Proposed Solution

We present a system under test (SUT) composed by an OLAP engine, a key-value database for persistent cube data according to the business scenarios of TPC-DS benchmark. Since the relational data model does not have linear scalability versus a pressing need for the analysis of large volumes of data, a few studies addressed OLAP benchmarking of NoSQL systems [21] [22] [23]. LinkedIn has built an OLAP engine: Avatara on Hadoop, which has been powering several analytics features on the site for the past two years [24].

Future benchmarks for big data analysis need consider how to support OLAP multidimensional model and adapt TPC benchmarks for NoSQL database systems. Thus, our work may be viewed more like TPC-DS benchmark testing proposition for key-value store systems. The proposition focuses on multidimensional implementation for big data analytics [2] [6]. We aim at integrating the classical, well-known benefits of the cube model with big data store infrastructures to achieve low latency OLAP queries in NoSQL database systems [28].

Main contribution of this paper is in answering how to build and store multidimensional data on top of big data systems and how to extend typical OLAP operators and parallel OLAP query processing on distributed key-value data store systems. Key points are summarized as followings.

1. The OLAP engine built on suitable NoSQL databases can embrace large scale cuboids repositories. We choose HBase for distributing cube data storage and improve stability by its offering a fine-grained fault tolerance model.
2. The engine can scale out seamlessly and provide different levels of concurrency. We propose a framework to allow building an event-driven concurrent system based on Akka actor model [7]. As such, OLAP query plan execution can be split into small parts for concurrent running on distributed nodes.
3. To verify the OLAP engine solution, experiments are taken with TPC-DS data which will be enriched with semi-structured and unstructured data components to become a big data benchmark called BigBench [8].

1.2 Paper Organization

In Section 2 we review related OLAP logical model design approaches and cube modeling techniques for TPC-DS schema. In Section 3, after illustrating proposed OLAP engine architecture, we show how to convert the snowflake data model into a multidimensional model based on array-based representation. When the analysis engine executing, the actor concurrency pattern and immutable event messages are heavily used for scalability and fault tolerance. We carry out a group of experiments to identify its performance bottlenecks on NoSQL databases based on TPC-DS data in Section 4. Finally, we summarize the mechanism of our OLAP engine implementation and present future works in Section 5.

2   Related Work

2.1   OLAP for Big Data

There are two fundamental OLAP engines for big data analytics: Relational OLAP (ROLAP) and Multidimensional OLAP (MOLAP). As for ROLAP, scenarios for big data analysis have been investigated in Hive [5]. ROLAP is designed to leave the data where it is and defer processing until it is actually queried. It becomes slow because of running complex map reduce jobs that consist of grouping and joining large data sets. As for MOLAP, the preprocessing and storage demands of a pure MOLAP approach are overwhelming either. Therefore, we have to make a compromise between the preprocessing costs of real time analytics and the usability of batch processing.

To make appropriate tradeoffs, we choose MOLAP rather than ROLAP as the underlying logical model. MOLAP aggregates the multidimensional data in the form of cuboids. Conceptually, the data cube consists of the base cuboid, the finest granularity view containing the full complement of d dimensions (or attributes), surrounded by a collection of 2^{d-1} cuboids that represent the aggregation of the base cuboid along one or more dimensions. Our solution is to pre-aggregate base cuboid in batch processing of cube data, and to aggregate other cuboids at runtime according to user queries [28]. To keep space usage efficient, only base cuboid data are stored, other cuboids are created in memory by user query requests.

2.2   Cube Modeling for TPC-DS

TPC-DS benchmark models the decision support functions of a retailer with a constellation schema with 7 fact tables and 17 shared dimensions. Its workload covers 99 queries classified into four classes: reporting queries, ad-hoc decision support queries, interactive OLAP queries, and extraction queries [9].

We can consider cube modeling based on two baselines for TPC-DS schema: 1) requirement driven: according to Kimball's "first principles", the design of TPC-DS cubes should be based on analysis of benchmark query templates, e.g. based on the knowledge of the application area and the types of queries the users are expected to pose [10]. 2) Data driven: like OLAP cubes construction based on queries proposed in [11], the logical cube construction may be based on the use of functional dependency involved in TPC-DS schema.

In this paper, we adopt TPC-DS queries as an optimization method rather than a logical cube design method. We combine the cube design and related queries to find the base cuboid data for each fact table and cache the data in memory at runtime so that other cuboids can be generated on the fly. As such, it is meaningful to think that an OLAP query returns a cuboid or the combination of some underlying cuboids.

Two types of cubes can be used to model TPC-DS schema: hypercubes and multicubes. We adopt multicubes and define 7 cube models for TPC-DS fact tables. The number of dimensions emerging from each distribution channel in TPC-DS is different. The *Catalog Sales* cube has 11 dimensions, *Web Sales* cube has 11 dimensions and *Store Sales* cube has 8 dimensions. Hierarchies of dimensions can be divided into four classes: *geography information, date, time* and *target market* (Table 1). In this paper, we illustrate the cube data construction on *Store Sales* cube and its related queries.

Table 1. Dimensions with hierarchies in TPC-DS

	Geography	Target Market	Date	Time
Store	√	√		
Call Center	√	√		
Website	√	√		
Warehouse	√			
Customer				
Customer Address	√		√	
Date_Dim			√	
Time_Dim				√

Tens of measures in TPC-DS can be grouped into 8 categories, namely *quantity, price, cost, discount related, tax, charges, cash flow related* and *profit* (Table 2). At the same time, plenty of calculated measures, which are derived by one or more current measures, are also proposed, such as *gross profit margin, net profit margin, average price, total cost*, etc.

Table 2. Categories of measures in TPC-DS

Categories of Measures	Measures
Quantity	Unit Sold, Unit Returned, Inventory Quantity, etc.
Price	Unit Sales Price, Unit List Price, Extended Sales Price, Extended List Price
Cost	Wholesale Cost, Ship Cost, etc.
Discount related	Discount, Coupon
Tax	Sales Income Tax, Ship Income Tax, Net Paid Income Tax, etc.
Charges	Return Fee, Reversed Charge, etc.
Cash flow related	Net Paid, Refunded Cash
Profit	Net Profit/Loss

2.3   Cube Algebra for TPC-DS Queries

We should work with TPC-DS SQL queries to transform them into MDX-like ones in order to take full advantage of MOLAP conceptual structures (e.g., concept hierarchies and cuboids and their paths). Defining the language formally is out of scope of this paper; instead, we illustrate its flavor with some of TPC-DS queries. Internally, we will adopt MDX model at the conceptual level and provide a common APIs for cube algebra [13].

The cube keeps aggregate values for the Group-bys of every possible combination of dimensions. The combination of some certain Group-bys is called a cuboid, and all different combinations form a lattice structure according to their Group-bys selection. The top cuboid that named base cuboid can be used to compute all of other cuboids. So we build the cube with base cuboid only in construction stage while generate other cuboids in querying stage.

3   MOLAP System Implementation

Recently, there are some implementations of MOLAP based on NoSQL databases: [26] integrated traditional RDBMS with multidimensional index structure layered over a range partitioned key-value store to provide scalable multi-dimensional data infrastructure. [27] designed and tested a scalable and inexpensive transparent data cube for Spatio-temporal data. [22] transformed multidimensional arrays to pig data for optimizing Pig Latin queries. LinkedIn [24] provided the OLAP engine architecture to build many, small cubes stored in key-value stores. Generally these systems consist of two subsystems: cube computation and query serving

Similarly, we build our OLAP engine based on the Hadoop as shown in Fig. 1. The OLAP engine provides high throughput during batch cube computation and low latency during online query serving. It can run in a cluster in which there are two roles of nodes: one is Dispatcher Node, who maintains the task status and dispatches the tasks; the others are Worker Nodes that execute tasks and cache the partition data in-memory. This has several features that differentiate it from traditional MOLAP engines:

1. Parallel and distributed pre-aggregation. With Akka actor topology, it can build cube data and run OLAP operations in a MapReduce-like style. The loading method for the hash-based base cuboid is better for larger data sets under distributed environments [14]. Thus we use a designed hash key algorithm and implement the OLAP engine with actor programming model.
2. Bit-wise key compression method. To convert bit key from multi-dimensional members, we can use key-value database to store the cube with the high performance in reading and writing. When caching we minimize the memory storage size by caching the bit key only. This reduces both the data size by as much as over naively storing the data in its original format, and shortens the processing time by applying the binary operations.
3. The engine is optimized for low latency, and provides an in-memory distributed storage for cube data. This approach is derived from Resilient Distributed Datasets (RDDs), a distributed memory abstraction that lets programmers perform in-memory computations on large clusters in a fault-tolerant manner [16].

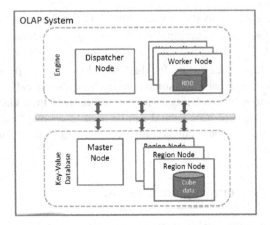

Fig. 1. OLAP system architecture build on HBase

In the following, we focus on how to build highly concurrent, distributed OLAP engine in Fig. 1 by:

- Distribute dynamically cubes data onto working nodes and parallelize OLAP queries (e.g. OLAP operations) into a concurrent model;
- Apply bitmap keys for operations such as aggregation, filter, group-by etc with respect to multi-thread concurrent access.

3.1   Cube Construction

The method in [15], used to derive multidimensional schema from requirements expressed in queries and relational schema, include two phases: cube building and query executing. Cube building includes 2 stages::

- Extracts dimensions and measures that are organized in a graph for each user query. The graph is crucial to infer base cuboid's metadata among associated queries;
- Validates each above graph according to the multidimensionality. To do so, a set of cuboids for user queries are defined, as such, we can summarize them into base cuboids for fact tables.

In the first stage, the dimensions and measures of each cuboid are decided by the related queries. Query 7 from TPC-DS queries is taken as an example:

```
select i_item_id, avg(ss_quantity) agg1, avg(ss_list_price)
agg2, avg(ss_coupon_amt) agg3, avg(ss_sales_price) agg4 from
store_sales, customer_demographics, date_dim, item, pro-
motion
  where ss_sold_date_sk = d_date_sk and
        ss_item_sk = i_item_sk and
        ss_cdemo_sk = cd_demo_sk and
```

```
        ss_promo_sk = p_promo_sk and
        cd_gender = '[GEN]' and
        cd_marital_status = '[MS]' and
        cd_education_status = '[ES]' and
        (p_channel_email = 'N' or p_channel_event = 'N') and
        d_year = [YEAR]
group by i_item_id
order by i_item_id
```

According to Query 7, a cube is defined. **Dimensions** are "i_item_id", "cd_gender", "cd_marital_status", "cd_education_status", "p_channel_email", "p_channel_event", "d_year". **Measures** are average of "ss_quantity", "average of ss_list_price", "average of ss_coupon_amt", and "average of ss_sales_price".

In the second stage, we merge all definitions of graphs that are inferred from related queries. Finally, we get a graph for the whole cube definition that is defined by the conjunction requirements of related queries.

To make OLAP operation work as MapReduce style [25], we divide a cube into multiple cube parts with the largest dimension. To keep sharing nothing, each part can be distributed to a worker node that works independently without communicating with the other nodes. Thus we adopt the denormalization method to put all dimension information into cube cells as the bitmap key (Fig.2) while the aggregation as the value. The cells will be distributed into different regions naturally by underlying HBase.

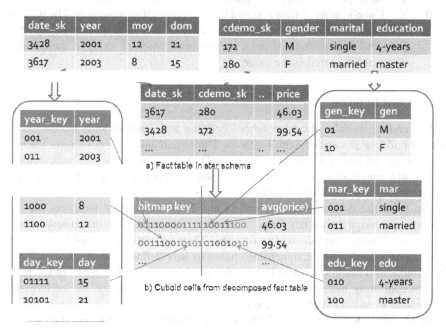

Fig. 2. Transform the fact table in star schema into base cuboid by denormalization

3.2   Key-Value Storage

[17] provides a multidimensional array method to organize star schema. The dimension members are stored with unique keys. The combinations of dimensions' keys are the indices of the dimension arrays which are used to determine the position of the measure values in the arrays. Next, each of the n-dimensional arrays is mapped into a linearized array by an array linearization function.

With this approach, each fact table of TPC-DS is first stored in a multidimensional array to remove the need for storing the dimension values. Then, the array is transformed into a linearized array. Finally, the linearized array is replaced by a bit-wise key compression method.

In this linearized function, each of dimensions has a mask to allocate its effective bits in the key. When new member added, the mask should be expanded if the dimension member size has reached the maximum of the effective bits. The masks can anti-linearize the measure keys to members' keys by XOR operation. This function costs less CPU times with bit operation instead of multiplication. We may append new dimension members by increasing member key and sign it in the mask when needed.

To store the array cuboid, we choose HBase, one of NoSQL database [18]. After converting the dimension array into key array, we put the cube data into HBase:

- The dimensions and dimension hierarchies are explicitly store with dimension name as row key. Furthermore, dimension member and its bit key are stored as key-value pairs. The reversed pairs are also stored as indices.
- The Cube's measure data is stored in each cuboid that is composed by different dimensions. The bit key for the cell of cuboid is taken as the row key. And the field and aggregation operation are combined into one string as the qualifier. The result is stored as the value.

3.3   Cube Building

Cube building includes the base cuboid building and other cuboids building. Base cuboid building is divided into 4 phases: Dimension initializing, records fetching, aggregating and saving. Data can be from any DBMS and will be sent to multi-actors to be handled concurrently in a round robin fashion. This is generally the longest part when loading large amounts of data.

We build the dimension instance first and fetch the distinct members for each attribute and assign them a key for cube metadata. Then store them into HBase as index and make all nodes load them after finished. Then we partition fact table tuples into small parts according to the dimension chosen by user defined policies. Let each node load tuples into multidimensional array. A tuple is represented as a cell in the multi-dimensional array indexed by the values of each of the attributes. In the following discussion, we use the hash based method [14].

Finally, the OLAP engine performs various granularity aggregation data calculations. Basic cuboids are constructed for fact tables by using multidimensional array technology. Other cuboids for various granularity aggregation data are derived from basic ones when these queried are executed at first time.

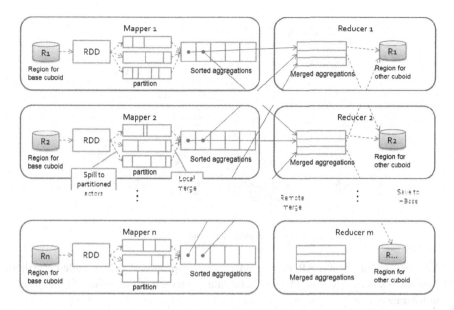

Fig. 3. Data flow of MapReduce to build other cuboid from base cuboid in the query execution

Base cuboid will be hold in memory and can be updated and refreshed by the dispatcher. For other cuboids, the dispatcher node schedules map tasks; each worker node sends the aggregated data to one reducer node that is appointed by the dispatcher.

3.4   Query Execution

When cube queries are submitted, the dispatch node will parse and decide whether the query uses existing cuboids or needs to construct new ones. If new cuboids required, the dispatcher send cuboid construction message to related worker nodes. Otherwise, it compiles the query into filter and expression, and then sends to related worker nodes.

Each worker node has a query executer that handles the message and sends back the hit cells to a node that accumulates all hit cells. The node transforms them into records with dimension member and returns them to the dispatcher.

As Fig. 4, the query executer manages amounts of mappers and reducers for the extractor and filter. There are two kinds of applying filters. The first one scans all the records and check whether it passes filtering constraints. If it does, send to reducers and take this record into account. Reducer helps to merge the result and sort. The second one tries to apply the filter to combine the dimensions that are not used in the filter. Thus each mapper will get an assembly key and try to fetch from HBase or memory cache. If found it, Mapper sends it to reducers. Here mappers and reducers can run on multi-threads, and give the benefits to be concurrent locally and remotely.. The overall parallelization obtains the efficiency. Cube data cannot be shared between actors.

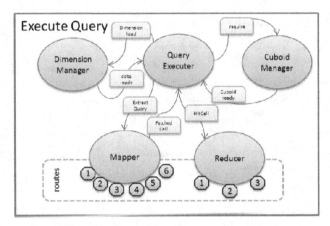

Fig. 4. Actor workflow for query executing

We implement the OLAP engine on a recently-proposed theory called Resilient Distributed Datasets (RDDs) [16]. It loads data in memory while offering fine-grained fault tolerance.

- Firstly, we set an RDD as a read-only, partitioned multidimensional array by the each region of HBase. It can be created by the worker from the base cuboid.
- Secondly, worker has enough information for RDD constructing from the message received. Thus it can materialize the RDD any time.
- Finally, the RDD's partitioning is controlled by the actors on worker nodes, and the RDD's automatically loaded when need.

4   Experiments

The whole workflow of our experiments is shown in Fig. 5. Clients (Remote Terminal Emulators) send cube build and OLAP query commands to Dispatcher which schedules the cube loading and constructing tasks and distributes them into Workers. After finished, Worker nodes return back the result to the dispatcher, then it merges results and renders to the client.

We use three data sizes of 1G, 10G and 100G and pre-load them into Hive. Based on query 7, 42, 52 and 55, we construct the *store sales* cube. The experiments utilized 3 physical worker nodes with 2 Intel Xeon CPU E5-2640@ 2.50GHz, 4 15000r/s SAS hard disk and 256G memories. OS of all is Ubuntu server 12.04. The network band width is 10Gbps. Configurations for experiments are based on out-of-the-box setting.

The test is divided into three sorts: correctness of OLAP engine implementation; cube building and OLAP querying performance on different scale data; and querying performance with 4, 8, and 16 workers. At last we compare the TPC-DS querys time between Hive and our proposed prototype.

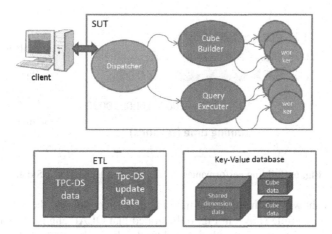

Fig. 5. Workflow for SUT

4.1   Implementation Verification Running

The correctness of OLAP engine is fundamental and the running result verification can be compared with SQL one with same data sets. We choose Query 7 which computes the average of quantity, list price, discount, and sales price for promotional items sold in stores where the promotion is not offered by mail or a special event. When restricting the results to gender as 'M', marital as 'S', year as 2000 and educational status as college, we got 5254 tuples, and the i_item_id data and related aggregation are same as the result from Hive SQL that is extracted from the same datasets besides the order of tuples is different since the prototype does not support sort operation.

4.2   Cube Building Performance

Loading test means constructing the cube from relational datasets. We experiment on 1 dispatcher node and 3 worker nodes. Each worker node has 32 actors who receives a partition of records and aggregate them and then save them. The details for handled data are showed in Table 3.

Table 3. Fact table record number, base cuboid cell number and region files size

	1G	10G	100G
records number	2,653,108	26,532,571	265,325,821
cube cell number	2,543,842	24,639,263	189,298,704
regions number	4*64M	64*64M	256*64M

We divide cube construction into four phases: 1) Initializing phase includes execute queries to fetch dimension members and save them into HBase. 2) Querying phase shows Hive's execution time for joining all tables. 3) Aggregating phase convert all records to bitwise key and aggregations. 4) Saving phase is to save all cells into HBase.

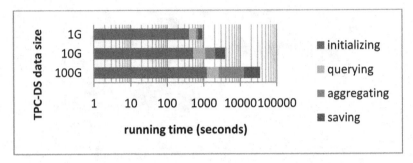

Fig. 6. Building performance on 1G, 10G and 100G TPC-DS data

The graph shows that the handling time increases according to the data scales. The aggregating phase time shows in Fig. 6 illustrated that OLAP engine does not act well as Hive since all the records are dispatched by the dispatcher node that is responsible to fetch the dataset. This is the bottleneck that we will try to set different fetch size for enhancement. Or we can execute hive query on the Hive gateway node for minimizing the network traffic. Since we do the test with out-of-the-box setting, the saving phase should be improved by optimizing configuration.

4.3 Querying Performance

For queries executing, we build RDD at first to scan the stored base cuboid and store them in partitions on worker nodes. Since HBase commonly does not keep each region server to store same number region, the owner with maximum regions will be the last one to finish the cache work. For 1G, 10G, 100G data, we got the cache time is 44, 255, 3997 seconds respectively. It implied that we should improve it in the following research activities by adopting some kinds of index.

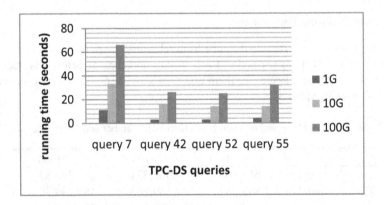

Fig. 7. Query performance on 1G, 10G and 100G TPC-DS data

After caching, the dispatcher compiles the queries into messages that composed by required cuboid and a set of filter keys and send them to worker nodes. After filtering, the results are sent to dispatcher that merges all the results. After all workers send their results, the dispatcher renders result to convert bitwise key to dimension members and returns them to the client.

We report cache times and queries time separately, and find that sharing data via RDDs greatly speeds up future iterations. The query time can be reduced between all worker nodes by given same number regions. The RDD just includes the base cuboid data and benefits OLAP operations that query other cuboids directly. Thus the cube data is only base cuboid size finally. We also can cache other cuboids dynamically for future iterations and we will research on the dynamical partition the other cuboids.

For experimenting, we first run query 7, 42, 52, 55 sequentially, i.e. each query is sent after the previous query's result is returned. Then we run them concurrently by sending them at once. And we find the query result is returned in the same order we send them. The reason is the caches are used exclusively since they are managed by actor which handles the data inquiries sequentially. It implied that more actors maybe improve the efficiency of scanning data.

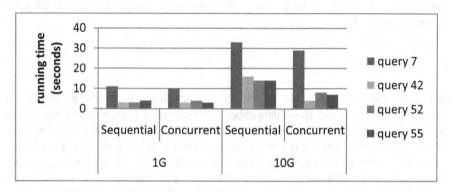

Fig. 8. Queries performance when running sequentially and concurrently on 1G, 10G data

From Fig.8, we see that the querying time is reduced relatively from 77 seconds that runs sequent to 48seconds that runs concurrently on 10G data. It infers we can optimize the performance by add more actors that leads heavier burden too.

4.4   Performance Comparative Analysis with Hive

Hive is deployed in out-of-the-box setting on three data nodes and same results are returned in experimenting on TPC-DS queries 7, 42, 52, and 55. We got the queries time of the prototype is generally about 50X times quicker than Hive.

Table 4. Comparing query performance on 10G TPC-DS data

	1G	10G	100G
query 7	14X	24X	19X
query 42	53X	49X	48X
query 52	53X	56X	50X
query 55	40X	56X	39X

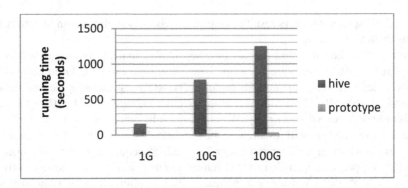

Fig. 9. Comparing query performance on 10G TPC-DS data

Sincerely, our prototype of OLAP engine has pre-aggregated the fact table data and kept partition in memory. In this way, the engine may support interactive OLAP operations on big data.

5   Conclusion

This article presents a feasible way to build multidimensional OLAP engines on NoSQL database systems. Basic data cubes are constructed from involved queries for fact tables by using multidimensional array technology, and cuboids for various granularity aggregation data are derived with basic ones at running time by using distributed and parallel dynamic cube data load workers. Basic cuboids are transformed into linearized arrays which are replaced by bit-wise keys suitable for key-values data stores. The OLAP engine implemented with Resilient Distributed Datasets (RDDs) can perform most computations in memory and cache the aggregation data in memory for quickening the interactive responds on large-scale data while offering fine-grained fault tolerance. The implementation has been successful in most of its original goals. The features provided by the prototype enable fast computation of results for some TPC-DS queries. The update of cube data will be touched in future.

From experiment results, we found the cube building and cuboids caching technologies need to be improved in various ways. For example, it is better to use MapReduce functions to creating basic cuboids from Hive tables and store them in the HBase. This will resolve the dispatcher's bottleneck found in above experiments. Another key for performance is to use distributed high-dimension index for interactive OLAP queries [12].

We reported performance results of building and querying against 4 TPC-DS queries for various data volumes. In the future more data schemas and different cluster parameter setting will be included into experiments. We investigated only the execution times in this paper. During experiments we also measured for business question, I/O costs of MapReduce tasks, the cost of data transfer for remote messages. By investigating these data, we envision the implementation of the MOLAP engine for handling most of queries with fully TPC-DS dimensionality on cloud systems.

Acknowledgements. This work was supported by national high-technology programs (2008ZX01045-004-01, 2009ZX01045-004-001 2009CB320706).

References

1. Evelson, B.: It's the dawning of the age of BI DBMS. Technical report (2011), http://www.forrester.com
2. Cuzzocrea, A., Il-Yeol, S., Karen, C.D.: Analytics over large-scale multidimensional data: the big data revolution. In: Proceedings of the DOLAP, pp. 101–103. ACM (2011)
3. Melnik, S., et al.: Dremel: interactive analysis of web-scale datasets. Proceedings of the VLDB Endowment 3(1), 330–339 (2010)
4. Corbett, J.C., et al.: Spanner: Google's globally-distributed database. In: Proceedings of the10th USENIX Symposium on OSDI, pp. 251–264 (2012)
5. Xin, R., et al.: Shark: SQL and rich analytics at scale.arXiv preprint arXiv:1211.6176 (2012)
6. Chen, Z., Carlos, O.: Efficient OLAP with UDFs. In: Proceedings of the DOLAP, pp. 41–48. ACM (2008)
7. Turcu, A., Binoy, R.: Hyflow2: A high performance distributed transactional memory framework in scala (2012), http://hyflow.org/hyflow/chrome/site/pub/hyflow2-tech.pdf
8. Ghazal, A., Hu, M., Rabl, T., Raab, F., Poess, M., Crolotte, A., Jacobsen, H.A.: BigBench: towards an industry standard benchmark forbig data analytics. In: Proceedings of the SIGMOD (2013)
9. Poess, M., Nambiar, R.O., Walrath, D.: Why you should run TPC-DS: a workload analysis. In: Proceeding of VLDB, pp. 1138–1149. ACM (2007)
10. Cheung, D., Zhou, B., Kao, B., Lu, H., Lam, T., Ting, H.: Requirement-based data cube schema design. In: Proceedings of the CIKM, pp. 162–169. ACM (1999)
11. Niemi, T., Nummenmaa, J., Thanisch, P.: Constructing OLAP cubes based on queries. In: The Proceeding of DOLAP, pp. 9–15. ACM (2001)
12. Dehne, F., et al.: A Distributed Tree Data Structure For Real-Time OLAP On Cloud Architectures
13. Ciferri, C., Ciferri, R., Gómez, L.I., Schneider, M., Vaisman, A.A., Zimanyi, E.: Cube Algebra: A Generic User-Centric Model and Query Language for OLAP Cubes. International Journal of Data Warehousing and Mining (2012)
14. Goil, S., Alok, C.: High Performance OLAP and Data Mining on Parallel Computers. Data Mining and Knowledge Discovery 1(4), 391–417 (1997)
15. Romero, O., Alberto, A.: Multidimensional Design by Examples. Data Warehousing and Knowledge Discovery, pp. 85–94. Springer, Heidelberg (2006)
16. Zaharia, M., et al.: Resilient distributed datasets: A fault-tolerant abstraction for in-memory cluster computing. In: Proceedings of the 9th USENIX Conference on NSDI (2012)
17. Li, J., Rotem, D., Srivastava, J.: Aggregation Algorithms for Very Large Compressed Data Warehouses. In: Proceedings of the VLDB, pp. 651–662. ACM (1999)
18. Taylor, R.C.: An Overview of the Hadoop/MapReduce/HBaseFramework and Its Current Applications in Bioinformatics. BMC Bioinformatics 11(suppl. 12), S1 (2010)
19. Dean, J., Sanjay, G.: MapReduce: Simplified Data Processing on Large Clusters. Communications of the ACM 51(1), 107–113 (2008)
20. Van Renesse, R., Dumitriu, D., Gough, V., et al.: Efficient Reconciliation and Flow Control for Anti-entropy Protocols. In: Proceedings of the LADIS. ACM (2008)

21. Moussa, R.: TPC-H Benchmark Analytics Scenarios and Performances on Hadoop Data Clouds. In: Benlamri, R. (ed.) NDT 2012, Part I. CCIS, vol. 293, pp. 220–234. Springer, Heidelberg (2012)
22. d'Orazio, L., Bimonte, S.: Multidimensional arrays for warehousing data on clouds. In: Hameurlain, A., Morvan, F., Tjoa, A.M. (eds.) Globe 2010. LNCS, vol. 6265, pp. 26–37. Springer, Heidelberg (2010)
23. Dutta, H., Kamil, A., Pooleery, M., et al.: Distributed Storage of Large-Scale Multidimensional Electroencephalogram Data Using Hadoop and HBase. In: Grid and Cloud Database Management, pp. 331–347. Springer, Heidelberg (2011)
24. Wu, L., Sumbaly, R., Riccomini, C., et al.: Avatara: Olap for web-scale analytics products. Proceedings of the VLDB Endowment 5(12), 1874–1877 (2012)
25. Wang, H., Qin, X., Zhang, Y., Wang, S., Wang, Z.: LinearDB: A relational approach to make data warehouse scale like MapReduce. In: Yu, J.X., Kim, M.H., Unland, R., et al. (eds.) DASFAA 2011, Part II. LNCS, vol. 6588, pp. 306–320. Springer, Heidelberg (2011)
26. Nishimura, S., Das, S., Agrawal, D., et al.: MD-HBase: design and implementation of an elastic data infrastructure for cloud-scale location services. In: Distributed and Parallel Databases, pp. 1–31 (2012)
27. Zhizhin, M., Medvedev, D., Mishin, D., et al.: Transparent Data Cube for Spatiotemporal Data Mining and Visualization. In: Grid and Cloud Database Management, pp. 307–330. Springer, Heidelberg (2011)
28. Lehene, C.: Low Latency "OLAP" with Hbase, HBaseCon (2012), http://www.slideshare.net/Hadoop_Summit/low-latency-olap-with-hadoop-13386744

PRIMEBALL:
A Parallel Processing Framework Benchmark for Big Data Applications in the Cloud

Jaume Ferrarons, Mulu Adhana, Carlos Colmenares, Sandra Pietrowska,
Fadila Bentayeb, and Jérôme Darmont

Université de Lyon (Laboratoire ERIC)
Université Lumière Lyon 2 – 5 avenue Pierre Mendès-France
69676 Bron Cedex – France
`first_name.last_name@univ-lyon2.fr`

Abstract. In this position paper, we draw the specifications for a novel benchmark for comparing parallel processing frameworks in the context of big data applications hosted in the cloud. We aim at filling several gaps in already existing cloud data processing benchmarks, which lack a real-life context for their processes, thus losing relevance when trying to assess performance for real applications. Hence, we propose a fictitious news site hosted in the cloud that is to be managed by the framework under analysis, together with several objective use case scenarios and measures for evaluating system performance. The main strengths of our benchmark definition are parallelization capabilities supporting cloud features and big data properties.

Keywords: Benchmark, Cloud Computing, Parallel Processing Framework, Big Data, Real Data.

1   Introduction

We are currently living through an information revolution that has undoubtedly brought a massive increase in the volume of data being produced and stored worldwide. In this Internet age, where the world creates 2.5 exabytes of data every day [1], traditional approaches and techniques for data analysis proved limited because some lack parallelism, and most lack fault tolerance capabilities. Therefore, in recent years, many platforms for parallel processing have been created so as to satisfy this need. These platforms provide frameworks for storing, accessing, updating and deleting data efficiently in computer clusters, ensuring fault tolerance and making the whole process transparent to users. Examples of such systems include Google's BigQuery [2] and Apache's Hadoop [3].

In this context, the terms "big data" are used for referring to digital information that comes in high volume, velocity and variety [1]; and the systems that make use of this type of data for achieving profitable objectives can be referred to as big data applications. Several examples of big data applications can be found

R. Nambiar and M. Poess (Eds.): TPCTC 2013, LNCS 8391, pp. 109–124, 2014.

in the areas of capital market, risk management, retail, social media analysis and meteorology. This kind of applications, beside requiring high parallel processing capabilities for analysis, also needs a good and scalable infrastructure capable of adapting quickly to an increment in computing or storage needs. Therefore, many big data applications are being deployed in the cloud so as to allow fast adaptability and flexibility.

Given the recent increase of big data applications in the cloud, and the use of parallel processing frameworks for dealing with the technical issues implied by the use of clusters and large amount of complex data, it has become important to fix standards so as to allow accurate comparisons of these frameworks. Several benchmarks already exist for measuring a system's parallelization capabilities, cloud features or big data analysis abilities, but none of them offers direct means of accurately measuring: 1) the three of them 2) in a real-life context.

Thus, following the principles defined by Folkerts et al. [4], we propose the specifications of PRIMEBALL to position it as a complete and unified benchmark for assessing a system's performance w.r.t. two main axes involved in the context of big data applications hosted in the cloud: parallel processing frameworks and cloud computing service providers. PRIMEBALL also aims to emulate common usages of cloud services, data manipulations and data transfers.

The remainder of this position paper is organized as follows. Section 2 reviews existing benchmarks similar to PRIMEBALL and motivates its design. Section 3 provides an overview of PRIMEBALL. Then, Sections 4, 5 and 6 detail the specification of PRIMEBALL's components, i.e., its dataset, workload, and properties and metrics, respectively. Finally, Section 7 concludes this paper and provides future research leads.

2   Related Work

Among the standard TPC benchmarks, TPC-DS, a decision support benchmark that models several generally applicable aspects of a decision support system, including queries and data maintenance [5], is closely related to data analytics we target at. However, although it can generate high volumes of data, its underlying business model is a classical retail product supplier, thence its dataset could not fully qualify as big data-oriented because of a lack in structural variety.

MalStone is benchmark for data intensive computing and analysis [6]. It features MalGen, a synthetic data generator that produces large datasets to perform benchmarking. Data is designed to assess systems from the parallel processing point of view. Data is generated probabilistically following specified distributions.

Cloud Harmony measures the performance of cloud providers as black boxes [7]. The tests performed are mainly focused on assessing hardware performance or specific technologies. Cloud Harmony actually aggregates the results of benchmarks that existed before.

The Yahoo! Cloud Serving Benchmark (YCSB) is a framework to facilitate performance comparisons among cloud database systems [8] that mainly focuses on key-value stores such as Dynamo [9]. YCSB defines several metrics and workloads to measure the behavior of the systems in different situations, or the same system when using different configurations.

Finally, the Statistical Workload Injector for MapReduce, or SWIM benchmark, is an open source benchmark that enables rigorous performance measurement of MapReduce systems [10]. It contains suites of workloads of thousands of jobs, with complex data, arrival, and computation patterns, and therefore provides workload-specific optimizations. SWIM is currently integrated with Hadoop.

We provide in Table 1 a synthetic comparison of all the above-mentioned benchmarks' properties, as well as PRIMEBALL's as a point of reference.

Table 1. Comparison of Benchmark Features

	TPC-DS	MalStone	Cloud Harmony	YCSB	SWIM	PRIMEBALL
Real data	~	No	~	No	No	Yes
Real workload	Yes	No	~	No	Yes	Yes
Parallel processing	Yes	Yes	Yes	Yes	Yes	Yes
Hardware-oriented	No	No	Yes	No	No	No
MapReduce-oriented	No	No	No	No	Yes	~
Cloud properties	~	Yes	No	Yes	Yes	Yes
Complex data	No	No	Yes	No	Yes	Yes
Big data	~	Yes	Yes	Yes	Yes	Yes
Technology-indep	Yes	Yes	Yes	No	No	Yes

The first property we compare is whether the data processed by a benchmark is produced artificially or extracted from a real environment. Only PRIMEBALL offers the possibility to work with wholly real data, with the aim to better simulate real applications including facets of the problem difficult to emulate when using random distributions to produce data. Although some of the benchmarks used in Cloud Harmony do use real data, most of them are actually processing artificial data. There are also in between positions such TPC-DS which produces data artificially but trying to follow the structure of a real environment. Proposing a real workload is the second property we selected. A benchmark system bearing this property is executing real-world operations to better simulate a production environment. PRIMEBALL, SWIM and TPC-DS execute only tasks that are closely related to real-world workloads. Moreover, some benchmarks in Cloud Harmony also execute tasks that are common in real environments but not all, for that reason has been marked with a tilde.

The next property is satisfied by all analyzed benchmarks, i.e., they are all aimed at assessing parallel processing. By contrast, Cloud Harmony is the only benchmark that assesses the performance of specific pieces of hardware. For example, it has benchmarks for measuring CPU performance, memory I/O and disk I/O. The other benchmarks can give a notion of the performance of specific parts of the hardware, but are not that specific.

The MapReduce-related property refers to benchmarks aiming at measuring the quality of a system in terms of the performance obtained when executing MapReduce tasks. SWIM is the only benchmark that is uniquely dedicated to MapReduce. However, if PRIMEBALL is implemented using MapReduce tasks, it can measure performance through them too. Cloud properties refer to the prominent features of cloud computing. All benchmarks but TPC-DS and Cloud Harmony are designed to measure properties such as vertical and horizontal scalability, consistency, etc. (cf. Section 6.1). Even though TPC-DS can be used, e.g., to measure the scale up of a distributed SQL database but it is not its purpose. On the other hand, PRIMEBALL has been designed as well to be able to assess this kind of properties.

Complex data properties describe the benchmarks that are oriented to execute procedures using complex data structures to assess the system under test (SUT). TPC-DS implements a classical data warehouse with numerical and textual values. MalStone only aims to generate a big dataset as a log file and measures system response while processing it, thus the data processed is not complex. The same is true for YCSB, which assesses the performance of key-value stores. Values can be complex, but they are not processed, only stored. The other benchmarks, including PRIMEBALL, include complex data in some of their procedures. Big data properties describe the benchmark systems that involve analytical aspects over large amounts of data. All benchmarks have analytical situations involving large amounts of data. PRIMEBALL has specifically been designed to satisfy this property. TPC-DS has been marked with a tilde because it can be used for this purpose but it depends mainly on the size of data used.

Finally, technology independence describes the systems the are designed to work with several kinds of technologies. YCSB and SWIM do not fulfill this property, because YCSB is oriented to analyze the performance of key-value stores only; and SWIM only assesses MapReduce procedures, and thus only makes sense when the SUT is able to execute them. The other benchmarks, including PRIMEBALL, can be used in environments that are not constrained by a given technology.

3   PRIMEBALL Overview

3.1   Application Model

PRIMEBALL's contextual application is set around New Pork Times: a fictitious on-line information service including international news, current affairs, documentaries, science, health and lifestyle sections. It is constantly updated and available 24-hours all around the world. New Pork Times hosts articles and multimedia documents about the latest news, as well as a large archive of past information.

All of these data are stored in a system called New Pork Times' News Hub (NPT-NH), which resides in a cluster hosted by some cloud service provider. This cluster is managed by a framework for parallel data processing and provides a remote storage that allows the user to access the files in the cluster without having to worry about their distribution in nodes. This storage system allows the user to insert and update data, and also to execute batch processes for analyzing/processing the data.

3.2 PRIMEBALL Features

This section lists what PRIMEBALL is/does and does not, so that its position, notably w.r.t. state of the art benchmarks (Section 2), is clear.

On one hand, PRIMEBALL:

- is a benchmark. It aims to compare the performance of the parallel processing framework under test with respect to several meaningful metrics;
- is cloud-oriented. The obtained results could also be used to compare:
  - cloud platforms as parallel processing frameworks,
  - service providers executing systems using the same cloud platform;
- is repeatable. All the proposed experiments are designed to lead to the same results if they are executed under the same conditions;
- is portable. The benchmark has been designed to be implemented in different cloud platforms.
- does define a set of operations that is meaningful in the context of parallel processing and cloud computing;
- does define performance metrics that are oriented to measure cloud properties. The criteria to assess each metric are also defined;
- does define data relationships. We provide a description of the information stored in the SUT to be processed during the benchmark run.

On the other hand, PRIMEBALL does not:

- define technical execution details. It defines guidelines, but given that SUTs can be very different, the relevance of results is tightly related to implementation details;
- define expected performance results. No absolute value is provided as a comparison point, given that they are subject to implementation details;
- compare data retrieval or processing algorithms;
- define a storage schema. However, we define how data are physically stored.

Thence, PRIMEBALL is the first cloud-oriented unified benchmark aiming to assess all the elements involved in cloud-based big data application systems.

4 PRIMEBALL Dataset

For using PRIMEBALL, it is necessary to implement NPT-NH (Section 3.1). Therefore, the following subsections contain a technical description of its architecture, the type of data it contains and the operations performed onto data by means of batch processes, such as metadata extraction.

4.1   Types of Files to be Hosted

The system's database shall hold only three types of files. However, there can be many files of the same type. The three types of files follow.

- General information (XML): This set of files comprise the many XML documents that describe the standard information stored by NPT-NH, i.e., information about authors, the actual news, and so on. Section 4.2 describes the conceptual schema of this information.
- Media files (binary): Some articles make references to these files, which can be either audio or video documents.
- Metadata (XML): Several metadata for information retrieval and other tasks are extracted from the other two types of files by internal algorithms, for further querying. These metadata must be persisted as XML files in the system.

4.2   PRIMEBALL Schema

The system must hold as XML files data about the following entities:

- articles: the actual news articles;
- topics: the topics an article may belong to;
- keywords: sets of words that roughly describe the content of an article;
- languages: marks for indicating what language/dialect an article is written in;
- authors: people who write the articles;
- journalists: authors who work in journals and make interviews;
- professionals: specialists in some topic who write special analyses;
- countries: information about countries authors might be citizens of or work in;
- dates: information about the day of the year when an article was written;
- media: reference to a media file with some internal comments.

The conceptual schema of this dataset is featured in Figure 1. Its actual implementation depends on the framework for parallel data processing to be benchmarked and its capabilities for storing data.

4.3   Initial Data

To create an initial corpus for populating NPT-NH, PRIMEBALL shall come bundled with a crawler that extracts, transforms and loads information from one or more real world news hub akin to New Pork Times (a famous news site may come to mind). The crawler fetches information about news published during a requested period of time, which is recommended to be set up as the last 40 years. Moreover, it must also extract information about authors, media files available, and metadata about the articles relevant to the system's architecture. Due the big data properties of the benchmark, it is recommended to fetch at least

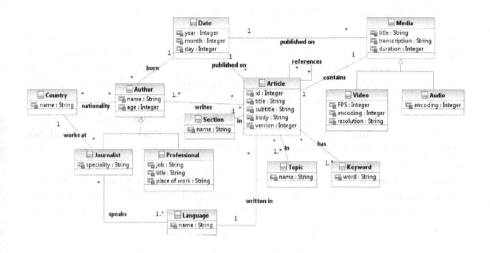

Fig. 1. Conceptual Schema of PRIMEBALL's Dataset

100 TB of data for running the tests. Although, depending on the environment to be benchmarked it might be required to use higher amounts of data. The benchmark can virtually scale up to 1 PB.

Once the corpus has been fetched, it can be sliced at will for selecting any scale factor for the initial data population. However, it is important to bear in mind that if the whole corpus is used in the initialization phase, then it will not be possible to perform updates or scale operations, since there will not be extra data available.

4.4   Metadata Processes

When data are loaded, it is necessary to run algorithms that extract some metadata from the files and build the structures for the following information retrieval tasks performed by NPT-NH:

– run a Hidden Markov Model [11] speech recognition algorithm on media files for transcribing the speech to text;
– compute the TF-IDF measure for all articles and transcriptions, as specified in the CDI IDF algorithm [12];
– compute the page rank of articles, as specified in the weighted pagerank algorithm [13];
– perform a topic extraction routine on articles and transcriptions, as specified in the Latent Dirichlet Allocation algorithm [14].

These algorithms have to be implemented as described in the cited references and adapted to be run in the cluster managed by the parallel data processing framework.

4.5   Data Scaling and Maintenance

This section describes the processes performed for updating and scaling data in NPT-NH. Basically, these processes are executed integrally as batch tasks. New Pork Times' authors write new articles every day. Articles have to be placed in NPT-NH for allowing access to users. New authors may also come in. The following scaling tasks have to be performed by the system. New data has to be obtained as progressive slices of PRIMEBALL's corpus, making sure that the data was not already inserted. Once new data are inserted, the system has to extract the necessary metadata from them so as to ensure that subsequent queries can be performed.

More specifically, when new information is inserted, it is necessary to recalculate some structures used for information retrieval. Thus, PRIMEBALL contains an implemented procedure for recomputing both TF-IDF metrics from all the documents and topics for all articles.

5   PRIMEBALL Workload

5.1   Query Set

This section contains the set of queries that are typically performed by NPT-NH users and that must be used for testing the performance of any given parallel data processing framework. These queries must be performed over the dataset defined in Section 4 and involve the most important aspects of performance. Although the following set of queries is not finite, it covers a wide range of classes from Figure 1, the relationships between them; it is applicable and enables to successfully measure performance.

One first subset of queries concerns the most common and hottest topics published in the system. The user might be interested in this information in order to know what kind of issues are the most frequently described in a certain interval of time, and therefore attract attention.

1. Articles containing the most frequent bigrams, sorted by pagerank.
2. Articles published during a time interval I, sorted by topics. The output contains pairs of article title and topic.
3. Most frequently used words by a journalist J from each country in the world during a certain time interval I. The output is compound by a list of countries, each one with keywords.
4. Rank of the keywords used in the articles published on an exact date D.
5. Most frequently used keywords in month M and year Y.

Furthermore, in order to evaluate how topics evolve w.r.t. time, it is necessary to include the various time measures in a second subset of queries.

6. Most frequently used keywords on day D and two different years Y_1 and Y_2, sorted by descending count.
7. Articles published on date D with the greatest number of references to the previous year.

8. Articles related to a topic T very frequently referenced lately, i.e., in a time interval I ending at the current date.
9. Journalists and professionals who wrote an article on the same month, on the same topic, sorted by days.

Finally, to analyze the diversity of articles and compare them w.r.t. their source, one should consider the following, eventual group of queries.

10. Articles written by X journalists in a specific time interval I that have at least Y common topics.
11. Rank of the languages in which articles are written. The output consists in pairs (language, number of articles).
12. Articles written by an author A from a given country C that best match a search term S.
13. Documents that best match another document published on the same day and month, but one year later.
14. Articles that focus on the same topic, but have been written by different journalists who were born before and after a given year Y.

5.2   Test Protocol

We present in this section different scenarios to help actually benchmark a system. To define them, a default scale factor SF is used. A dataset of scale factor SF is a set of articles and corresponding metadata having a total size of SF GB.

Scenario 1. This scenario simulates the evolution of the system along time, in terms of data operations and queries.

Initial state. The system contains a dataset with a specified scale factor SF.

Operations

1. Execute queries 4, 7 and 14 from the generic query set (Section 5.1) choosing as date, e.g., September 12, 2001.
2. Double the volume of the dataset according to scenario 7.
3. Repeat the queries executed in step 1, for the same date and another one, e.g., November 5, 2008.

Scenario 2. This scenario simulates an extreme situation: a very famous article has been published with many mistakes and publishers are correcting it constantly. Their main concern is to deliver a consistent view of the article to people. Here, we are interested in measuring how many times the article is read in the older versions after being read once in the new version.

Initial state. The system contains a dataset with a specified scale factor SF.

Operations

1. Initiate a thread performing 100 queries per second to retrieve the given article.
2. Start another thread updating the same article every 5 seconds.

Scenario 3. This scenario simulates node failures in terms of network reachability. Here, we are interested in knowing how many nodes can be removed from the cluster before some data become unreachable.

Initial state. The system contains a dataset with a specified scale factor SF.

Operations

1. Execute all queries from the generic query set (Section 5.1) sequentially.
2. Remove a node and reiterate step 1.

Scenario 4. This scenario aims to measure the concurrency offered by the system while accessing data.

Initial state. The system contains a dataset with a specified scale factor SF.

Operations. Execute the following process 300 times and count the number of inconsistencies.

1. Start 10 threads executing the whole generic query set (Section 5.1).
2. Start 5 threads each of them performing:
   (a) updates in articles: 10 per second;
   (b) removing articles: 10 per second;
   (c) adding articles: 10 per second.

Scenario 5. The objective of this scenario is to simulate analysis procedures over the dataset.

Initial state. The system contains a dataset with a specified scale factor SF.

Operations. Execute queries uniformly selected from the following.

1. Top 10 articles seen each month in 2010.
2. Average number of pages per article for each journalist in the system.
3. Average age of publishers and standard deviation.
4. Maximum number of versions of an article.

Scenario 6. The aim of this scenario is to initialize the system and make it ready for handling the information for New Pork Times.

Initial state. Empty storage system.

Operations. Execute the steps described in Section 4.3 to initialize the environment.

Scenario 7. This scenario is used to increase the volume of the dataset to simulate the fact that new articles are inserted over time.

Initial state. NPT-NH has a consistent state.

Operations. Execute the steps described in Section 4.5 for data scaling and maintenance.

6 PRIMEBALL Properties and Metrics

6.1 Properties and Performance Metrics

This section presents the metrics that we use to evaluate the performance of the SUT. We also define the different system properties that can be assessed using PRIMEBALL.

We first specify two main metrics. The first one is throughput. The throughput of the SUT for a given scenario is the total time required to execute it (scenarios are defined in Section 5.2). The second metric, price performance, takes price (Section 6.2) into account and is expressed as follows.

$$Price\ performance = \frac{Throughput}{Price}$$

Moreover, the set of operations that can be executed against the system in the context of New Pork Times is defined as follows.

- Read: Obtain one or more articles.
- Write: Create a new article or a new version, add new journalists, languages, topics...
- Update: Modify an existing article within the same version or modify the information related to a journalist.
- Delete: Remove inappropriate content.
- Search: Obtain articles by matching a search (a set of given words, topics, authors, dates...).

Using all these definitions, we can set the following properties.

Generic Cloud Properties

1. **Scale up:** ability of the system to handle more data when adding more computers while maintaining performance.
   - *Importance*: In the case of a news website, it is very important to be able to scale up the system. There are a lot of news added every day and the service must keep on performing the same.
   - *Measurement*: To measure this property, scenarios 4 and 5 (Section 5.2) must be executed twice, doubling the amount of data (SF) and the amount of nodes in the cluster the second time. Throughput increase ratio is the metric recommended for this property.

$$Throughput\ increase\ ratio = \frac{Throughput\ after}{Throughput\ before}$$

2. **Elastic speedup:** adding more computers to the cluster with the same amount of data results in better performance.
   - *Importance*: For New Pork Times, it is very relevant to know whether the system can offer a better performance when required, e.g., when there is a worldwide event with more people involved than usual looking for news and information. Thus, it is crucial to be able to maintain the quality of service even during peak demands.
   - *Measurement*: To measure this property, we propose to execute scenarios 2, 4 and 5 (Section 5.2) in order to observe throughput with the default cluster SF size. The metric we propose is also throughput increase ratio.

$$Throughput\ increase\ ratio = \frac{Throughput\ after}{Throughput\ before}$$

3. **Horizontal scalability:** ability of the system to distribute evenly the data load and workload among cluster nodes.
   - *Importance*: It is very useful to know up to what point one can exploit the current cluster and keep throughput in between some boundaries. In other terms, we determine what highest price performance can be achieved. It is very interesting in two senses:
     - upper bound: to answer the question "how many articles can the news website add into the system while keeping response time below 0.2 seconds";
     - lower bound: to optimize resource usage while fixing a performance lower bound. It might indeed be possible to reduce the number of nodes and offer the same user experience (response time).
   - *Measurement*: To assess this property, scenarios 4 and 5 (Section 5.2) must be executed and system throughput measured. Then, SF is increased and the process repeated. Again, throughput increase ratio can be used to evaluate this property. The closer it is to 1, the better is horizontal scalability.

$$Throughput\ increase\ ratio = \frac{Throughput\ after}{Throughput\ before}$$

4. **Latency:** time to execute a set of operations.
   - *Importance:* For New Pork Times, it is essential to be able to show news very quickly to users. If it takes too much time, users are going to look for a different website, thus a low latency is required.
   - *Measurement:* Latency of the SUT can be measured as the throughput when executing scenarios 4, 5 and 6 (Section 5.2).

5. **Durability:** ability of the system to retain information for a long period of time.
   - *Importance:* In the case of a news website, it is very important to ensure that no information is lost. Users have to be able to check and find information they have read previously.
   - *Measurement:* Scenario 1 (Section 5.2) is intended to measure data durability. We define the durability ratio as a metric for this purpose.

$$Durability\ ratio = \frac{Correct\ reads}{Total\ reads}$$

6. **Consistency and version handling:** two different readings of the same data at the same time should return the same value.
   - *Importance:* It is important for a website to give a consistent view of data to all users at the same time around the world. In the proposed model, There may be several revisions of an article, which has to be consistent for all readers.
   - *Measurement:* Using scenario 2 (Section 5.2), the performance of the system for this property can be measured using the consistency ratio as a metric.

$$Consistency\ ratio = \frac{Consistent\ reads}{Total\ reads}$$

7. **Availability:** data is accessible even when there are some inaccessible nodes.
   - *Importance:* It is very relevant for New Pork Times to guarantee the access to all the news stored in the system.
   - *Measurement:* Scenarios 3 and 6 (Section 5.2) aim to measure this property, thus the throughput of the SUT can be taken as a metric for this property.

8. **Concurrency:** the system has to be able to offer a service to different clients at the same time.
   - *Importance:* In New Pork Times, users can keep reading while publishers are adding news, and the system has to be able to handle the multiple operations of different natures at the same time.
   - *Measurement:* Given concurrent scenario 4 (Section 5.2), we propose two metrics:
     - system throughput;
     - concurrency ratio.

$$Concurrency\ ratio = \frac{Successful\ operations}{Total\ operations}$$

Complex Data Properties

9. **Path traversals:** ability of the system to link data from different parts of the schema using the defined relationships.
   - *Importance:* In the case of a news Web site environment, this property is very important to improve search experience.
   - *Measurement:* Queries 3, 4, 7, 10 and 12 (Section 5.1) from the generic query set involve following a path through different class relations to link concepts. The throughput of this type of queries is used to measure that property.
10. **Construction of complex results:** ability of the system to generate (semi)-structured output from the information system.
    - *Importance:* This property is very relevant to a news website, mainly to allow analysis over the contained data.
    - *Measurement:* The generic query set defined in Section 5.1 contains queries with complex results, i.e., queries 2, 3, 6 and 11. The throughput of these queries can be used as a metric for this property. Moreover, scenario 6 (Section 5.2) has to be used to measure this property.
11. **Polymorphism:** ability of the system to deal with type inheritances, i.e., treating types and subtypes of objects to compute query results.
    - *Importance:* Inheritance is a good way to deal with complex relationships between objects. For this reason, the performance of the system while executing these kinds of operations is very relevant.
    - *Measurement:* Fix a cluster and an initial workload, then execute and measure system performance while executing queries 3, 9, 12 and 15 (Section 5.1; all of them involve inheritance operations).

Big Data Properties

12. **Analysis:** ability of the system to generate summarized data and statistical information.
    - *Importance:* For a news website, having statistics such as how many times an article has been read, average words per article, etc., is very relevant.
    - *Measurement:* This property can be measured in terms of throughput while executing analytical scenario number 5 (Section 5.2).

Information Retrieval Properties

13. **Full text:** being able to search a single word in all documents simultaneously.
    - *Importance:* This property is very relevant to a news website to allow users searching information easily in the system.
    - *Measurement:* It can be measured in terms of throughput when searching for different terms, some famous, some normal and some strange, e.g., Obama, Higgs, Star Trek, Cleopatra, etc. Queries of this type are included in the generic query set (Section 5.1).

6.2 Pricing

In Section 6.1, we defined sytem performance w.r.t. time and cost. The main pricing factors involved in processing data in the cloud follow.

- Cloud provider: different cloud service providers may have different pricing policies.
- Number of instances and type: infrastructure used to execute PRIMEBALL.
- Required storage space: it is directly related to the scale factor used (Section 5.2).
- Platform inherent costs: operation, administration and maintenance.
- Execution time: time spent to run the tests.

The specific cloud provider model has to be applied to compute real cost.

7 Conclusions

We propose in this paper the specifications for PRIMEBALL, a complete and unified benchmark for measuring the characteristics of parallel cloud processing frameworks for big data applications. In front of the already existing benchmarking options, PRIMEBALL can be used as a guideline to build an integral solution for benchmarking could platforms. The real-life model adopted in PRIMEBALL is that of a fictitious news hub called New Pork Times, which is basically a fair approximation of a popular real-life news site. The general architecture and inner processes of the system are well-defined so as to allow an unambiguous implementation of the benchmark.

The workload applied on this news dataset is not only made of queries, but also of data-intensive batch processes. Moreover, we propose several use-case scenarios together with relevant metrics for assessing the framework's performance from different points of view, such as data availability or horizontal scalability. The novelty of our work lies in the fact that existing, related benchmarks measure parallelization capabilities, cloud features, big data analysis ability, but none of them combines all these properties while exploiting real-life data.

Future work on PRIMEBALL will be mainly focused on implementing a crawler for fetching and transforming real data from the Web to feed the benchmark's dataset. Distributing the built dataset online will improve the repeatability of the experiments. Moreover, the actual feasibility and relevance of PRIMEBALL shall be validated by actually implementing the benchmark in several cloud environments to obtain experimental results and by publishing performance comparison results. For instance, implementation in popular data processing frameworks such as Hadoop should be achieved.

Moreover, future extensions of the benchmark could include new scenarios that exploit different properties of cloud providers, such as vertical growth of the cluster, or new measures such as efficiency of bandwidth use. Actual experiments should also help refine the benchmark's workload.

References

1. IBM, What is big data? (2012), http://www-01.ibm.com/software/data/bigdata/
2. Sato, K.: An Inside Look at Google BigQuery, White paper (2012), https://cloud.google.com/files/BigQueryTechnicalWP.pdf
3. Shvachko, K., Kuang, H., Radia, S., Chansler, R.: The Hadoop Distributed File System. In: 26th IEEE Symposium on Mass Storage Systems and Technologies (MSST 2010), Incline Village, USA, pp. 1–10 (2010)
4. Folkerts, E., Alexandrov, A., Sachs, K., Iosup, A., Markl, V., Tosun, C.: Benchmarking in the Cloud: What it Should, Can, and Cannot Be. In: Nambiar, R., Poess, M. (eds.) TPCTC 2012. LNCS, vol. 7755, pp. 173–188. Springer, Heidelberg (2013)
5. Transaction Processing Performance Council (TPC), TPC Benchmark DS Standard Specification Version 1.1.0 (2012), http://www.tpc.org
6. Open Cloud Consortium, Generate synthetic site-entity log data for testing and benchmarking applications requiring large data sets (2009), http://code.google.com/p/malgen/
7. Cloud Harmony (2013), http://www.cloudharmony.com/benchmarks
8. Cooper, B.F., Silberstein, A., Tam, E., Ramakrishnan, R., Sears, S.: Benchmarking cloud serving systems with YCSB. In: 1st ACM Symposium on Cloud Computing (SoCC 2010), Indianapolis, USA, pp. 143–154 (2010)
9. DeCandia, G., Hastorun, D., Jampani, M., Kakulapati, G., Lakshman, A., Pilchin, A., Sivasubramanian, S., Vosshall, P., Vogels, W.: Dynamo: amazon's highly available key-value store. In: 21st ACM SIGOPS Symposium on Operating Systems Principles (SOSP 2007), pp. 205–220 (2007)
10. Chen, Y., Alspaugh, S., Ganapathi, A., Griffith, R., KatzThe, R.: Statistical Workload Injector for MapReduce (SWIM) (2013), https://github.com/SWIMProjectUCB/SWIM/wiki
11. Juang, B.H., Rabiner, L.R.: Hidden Markov models for speech recognition. Technometrics 33(3), 251–272 (1991)
12. Xu, M., Liang, H., Xin, L.: A Refined TF-IDF Algorithm Based on Channel Distribution Information for Web News Feature Extraction. In: Second International Workshop on Education Technology and Computer Science (ETCS 2010), Wuhan, China, vol. 2, pp. 15–19 (2010)
13. Wing, W., Ghorbani, A.A.: Weighted pagerank algorithm. In: Second Annual Conference on Communication Networks and Services Research (CNSR 2004), Fredericton, Canada, pp. 305–314 (2004)
14. Newman, D., Asuncion, A., Smyth, P., Welling, M.: Distributed algorithms for topic models. The Journal of Machine Learning Research 10, 1801–1828 (2009)

CEPBen: A Benchmark for Complex Event Processing Systems

Chunhui Li and Robert Berry

Aston University, Birmingham, U.K.
{lic5,r.f.berry}@aston.ac.uk

Abstract. Complex Event processing (CEP) has emerged over the last ten years. CEP systems are outstanding in processing large amount of data and responding in a timely fashion. While CEP applications are fast growing, performance management in this area has not gain much attention. It is critical to meet the promised level of service for both system designers and users. In this paper, we present a benchmark for complex event processing systems: CEPBen. The CEPBen benchmark is designed to evaluate CEP functional behaviours, i.e., filtering, transformation and event pattern detection and provides a novel methodology of evaluating the performance of CEP systems. A performance study by running the CEPBen on Esper CEP engine is described and discussed. The results obtained from performance tests demonstrate the influences of CEP functional behaviours on the system performance.

Keywords: Complex Event Processing, Performance Evaluation, Benchmark, Complexity, Throughput, Response Time.

1 Introduction

Computer systems are now used in almost every imaginable field from science to day-to-day activities of our lives. Meanwhile, sensors and mobile appliances are widely applied both in daily life and research for monitoring the environment. The amount of sensors and mobile appliances in one application can be extremely large and they could generate great volume of data, whose types can vary greatly. This tremendous increase to process and handle large quantities of information poses challenges for IT systems.

Complex event processing (CEP) are outstanding in processing large amount of data and responding in timely fashion. As society demand faster reactions to changing conditions, CEP systems are means to meet this demand. Applications in many domains have benefited from event processing technologies, e.g., active diagnostics, real-time operational decision, predictive processing, observation systems and information dissemination. Complex event processing engines provides three main functional capabilities: filtering, transformation and event patterns detection. A filter operation takes an event input and decides whether this event is to be selected for further processing. A transformation operation takes one or more input events and generates different output events that are

R. Nambiar and M. Poess (Eds.): TPCTC 2013, LNCS 8391, pp. 125–142, 2014.

based on them. Event patterns are templates specifying one of more combinations of events. An event pattern detection operation detects such templates [10].

Complex event processing systems has emerged in the last ten years, but performance management of such systems has not gain enough attention. Performance management ensures that performance goals and the promised level of service are consistently being met in an effective and efficient manner. Benchmarks are often created for exploring performance characteristics of an application under varying but controlled conditions. Performance reports can be found from various CEP venders, e.g. Oracle [2,3], Esper [1] and StreamBase [19]. Their methodologies in benchmarking CEP systems focus on scaling the load injection, but do not consider the impact of the types of queries on the performance of the systems. These queries registered in the system decide what functions the CEP system performs on events in the event processing. Therefore, the functional capabilities of a CEP system are critical. We propose the approach of evaluating the performance of CEP engines' functional behaviours on events and create the CEPBen benchmark for CEP systems.

In this paper, we present a benchmark of complex event processing systems focusing on complex event processing functional behaviours: filtering, transformation and event pattern detection. We describe our benchmark design and tests, as well as the factors influence performance measurements. We create a benchmark application with Esper complex event processing engine [1], an open source CEP engine. Lastly, we present and discuss the results obtained from performance tests on this benchmark application. The performance tests demonstrate that the degree of the complexity of CEP functional behaviours has impact on system performance. We believe that the CEPBen offers a flexible environment of exploring the influential factors of performance and the performance metrics for these factors.

2   The Benchmark

In this section, we present the benchmark CEPBen. The goals, the workload design and performance metrics of the CEPBen, the design and the implementation are described.

2.1   Goals and the Tested Systems

CEP delivers high-speed processing of events, identifying the meaningful events according to defined rules, and taking subsequent action in real time. The goal of this benchmark is to measure the efficiency of CEP engines' functional behaviours.

The Figure 1 illustrates the timeline of events in a CEP system and the system behaviours. Events occur at T_1, and transmit to the front end of the event

---

[1] EsperTech: http://esper.codehaus.org/

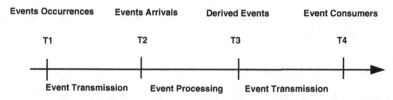

Fig. 1. The system behavior of an event processing system

processing engine at T_2. After being processed, derived events are generated at T_3 and sent back into the CEP engine for further processing or transmitted to event consumers. Event consumers receive the derived events at T_4.

Event transmission and event processing are crucial for the performance of a CEP system. Event sources and event processing engines influence event processing. Event sources are the resources of events, which influence the system by their schema, time, causality, aggregation and input rate. Event processing engines drive the whole system to provide satisfactory services in detecting events and their patterns and generating necessary messages for actions. Meanwhile, event transmission is much depending on networks, because event sources and event consumers usually have distributed features. Thus, the performance of networks plays an important role in such scenarios. Since we focus on the event processing behaviours in our benchmark, the performance of networks is not tested in our benchmark.

2.2 WorkLoad Design

To simplify the abstraction of the workload for performance tests, we propose a batched model for the event workload. The workload is designed to consist of event batches of variable size with varying interval times (depending on desired load). The Figure 2 describes that events from various event sources form the event cloud [16] and arrive in the CEP engine in batches .

The workload can scale in the following dimensions: 1) The number of event batches; 2) The number of events in a batch; 3) The Interval times between two event batches. The interval times in a workload generally arbitrarily distributed. The average time of the intervals can be changed as we vary the load. Short

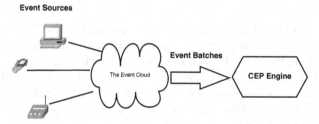

Fig. 2. The workload model of the CEPBen benchmark

intervals mean heavier workload in a time unit for the system, while long intervals mean less workload in a time unit.

2.3   Selection of Metrics

Throughput and response time are commonly applied metrics in measuring information systems. Throughput can be categorized into input throughput and output throughput in light of the independence feature of event producers and event consumers in CEP systems [10].

Suppose a workload with n event instances is sent into the event processing engine and m output events are generated after the event input are processed. The input throughput is measured by:

$$Input \quad Throughput = \frac{The\ Number\ of\ Input\ Events\ in\ the\ Period}{T_{Nth} - T_{1st-input}} \qquad (1)$$

$$Output \quad Throughput = \frac{The\ Number\ of\ Output\ Events\ in\ the\ Period}{T_{Mth} - T_{1st-output}} \qquad (2)$$

$T_{1st-input}$ and T_{Nth} are the start and the end of the sample period for measuring the input throughput. $T_{1st-output}$ and T_{Mth} are the start and the end of the sample period for measuring the output throughput after the system reaches steady state.

Response time is one of the performance metrics in the CEPBen. The measurement of response time will be described with the benchmark design.

2.4   Benchmark Design

The goal of complex event processing is to identify meaningful events and respond to them as quickly as possible. Three main functionalities are necessary to perform the event processing: filtering, transformation and event pattern detection. Our benchmark is designed to test the three main functional capabilities. Therefore, we believe our benchmark environment can be used to model the behaviours of a range of CEP applications.

Tests for Filtering. This group of tests focuses on filtering function of event processing systems. We create a query load of selection operations for the event processing engine. Before each event is about to be sent in to the event processing engine, the event is labelled with the system time T_{in}. When the event is selected according to the selection queries by the event processing engine, it is labelled with the current system time T_{out} . We measure such responsive behaviour of the system by the metric of response time:

$$T_{response} = T_{out} - T_{in} \qquad (3)$$

Tests for Transformation. This group of tests focuses on transformation function of event processing systems. We create a query load of join operations for the event processing engine. These operation will perform on events in one input stream and different input streams. An event is sent into the event processing engine at T_{in}. Join operation perform on two events (E_1 and E_2). Suppose E_2 is sent into the event processing engine later that E_1, that means $T_{2in} > T_{1in}$. The new output event is generated at system time T_{out}. The response time of transformation behaviour is defined as:

$$T_{response} = T_{out} - T_{2in} \tag{4}$$

Tests for Detecting Event Patterns. This group of tests focuses on the system behaviour of detecting event patterns. We create a query load of event patterns for the event processing engine. Suppose a system is targeted at an event E (labelled with the system time T_{target}) only when this event E happens in an event pattern. When all the required events for matching this pattern are detected, a new event responding to the event pattern detection is generated at the system time T_{out}. The response time of the pattern detection is defined as:

$$T_{respone} = T_{out} - T_{target}. \tag{5}$$

Factors. We identify the following factors that have an impact on the performance of a CEP system:

- The workload. Heavy workload challenges a CEP system's capability to handle large amount of events.
- The query load. Query load is the number of query statements in different test groups. Handling large sets of query statements efficiently is a challenge for CEP engines. CEP engines take time to process events against each query. It is expected that a larger number of query statements increases the total processing time and consumes more resources of the computer, and slows down the CEP system.
- The depth that query statements perform on event history. Transformation functionality produces composite events. The composite events can be formed based on different number of primitive events. An event pattern can involve more than one primitive event as well. We specify the number of primitive events that are used to produce a composite event and to match an event pattern as the depth of a query statement. The depth of query statements influences the performance of an CEP system. To process events against more-depth statements, the CEP engine need to catch and hold the required events temporarily, which is resource-consuming.
- The machine configuration where the event processing engine is run. The performance of a CEP system relies on the hardware configuration of the machine on which the CEP system runs.

2.5   Benchmark Implementation

We implement our benchmark on a performance-oriented framework shown in the Figure 3. The benchmark consists of several modules: the event generator, the input layer, the event processing engine, the output layer, the query module, the events consumers and the performance monitoring and analysis module. The event generator generates a workload for the CEP system. The input layer and an output layer are created as the front end and back end of the event processing engine. The event processing engine is the central component of this CEP system, as it performs complex event processing. The query module sets the operations for event processing engine. The event consumers are the users which consume derived events that are processed by the event processing engine. Performance monitoring and analysis collects performance data and generates performance report of this CEP system.

Applying the benchmark on CEP systems requires some programming work. Implementation of the event generator, input layer, output layer, query module and interfaces for performance measurement are depending on tested CEP systems.

Benchmarking Event processing Systems

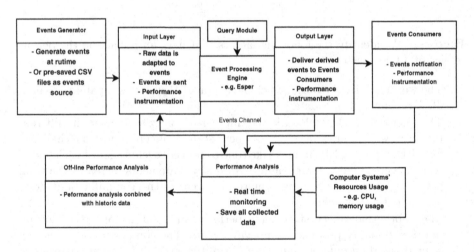

Fig. 3. The architecture of the benchmark

The Event Generator. The event generator is used for generating events according to desired load. It can be set to two different modes: generating events at runtime or reading events from saved comma-separated values (CSV) files. To overcome concerns about computer resources (e.g., memory consumption, CPU consumption), the event generator can be installed on remote machines and send events into event processing systems.

Generating events at runtime provides users flexibility to define the events data that they want to use. Users can either make some data according to the scenarios of simulations that they are interested in, or make random data for tests. Events volume, events types and events rate can be well defined and controlled.

Saved CSV files can be used as events feed to event processing systems. The adapters in the input layer convert CSV readings to event instances and send them to the event processing engine.

Input Layer and Output Layer. The input layer is the front end of the event processing engine component. Adapters convert events from various event sources into event instances that the CEP engine processes. Events senders send these events processed by adapters into the CEP engine. Both are implemented in this layer.

The output layer is used for delivering derived events from the event processing engine to events consumers. The derived events can be alerts from detecting certain events patterns, events to change configuration of the system, events to be processed again or events to be deleted. Derived events and events with new configuration information go through the events channel and arrive in the input layer to get processed.

Event Processing Engine. Event processing engine is the core component of an event processing system. CEP engines from different venders can be applied here. In our benchmark, the event processing engine connects to events sources via input layer, and outputs notification to events consumers via output layer.

Query Module. The query module is built for generating query statements to capture the events and events patterns. Generally, the query module should be implemented based on the type of query statements (i.e., selections, joins, windows, event patterns), the number of different type of query statements and an execution plan. As there is no standard event processing languages across CEP engines, the query module need to be implemented according to the event processing engine that users adopt.

Event Consumers. Event Consumers should be implemented according to the design of CEP systems. Because we focus on the behaviours of event processing engine, we implemented simple event consumers which subscribe events and generate text alerts when the events are detected in our benchmark.

Performance Monitoring and Analysis. Performance monitoring and evaluation needs instrumentation to gather data on executing systems and processes, techniques for data analysis and representation, theories and models which realistically represent computer systems and computer processes. In the benchmark, two modes of performance monitoring and analysis are designed: real-time and off-line mode. The performance of the system in a real time manner in every running performance test can be displayed. The off-line performance analysis is performed to compare the performance results which are obtained in performance tests.

2.6   Features of Flexibility of the CEPBen

The CEPBen has the following features of flexibility.

- It is able to present a varied workload for meet the requirements of different performance tests. Users can create events with their desired event properties, batch size, batch frequency.
- By setting the number of query statements and the depth of query statements, the benchmark presents varied degrees of application query complexity for investigating the system behaviours.

These features will help to explore a range of factors influencing the performance of CEP systems and a range of metrics to better show that performance.

3   Benchmark Demonstration and Results

3.1   Benchmark Application

To demonstrate the benchmark, we run our benchmark on Esper complex event processing engine. Event generator is configured to generate four types of events (EventA, EventB, EventC, EventD) for the workload. By default, we set event ID and timestamp property for each event. Other string properties for events are drawn from a string pool with a random process. The integer values in properties are generated randomly. The event structure is shown as following:

```
EventA (String eventID, long timeStamp, String attributeA)
EventB (String eventID, long timeStamp, String attributeB)
EventC (String eventID, long timeStamp, String attributeC1, int attributeC2)
EventD (String eventID, long timeStamp, int attributeD1, String attributeD2)
```

Input layer and output layer are programed on the Esper engine. Event consumers receive processed events from the engine and generate text alerts.

Three types of queries are implemented in the query module: Selection statements are created for tests of filtering functionality; Join statements are created for tests of transformation functionality; Event pattern statements are created for tests of event pattern detection functionality. The Event Processing Language (EPL) is the language of the Esper event processing. EPL is a SQL-like language with SELECT, FROM, WHERE, GROUP BY, HAVING and ORDER BY clauses [9]. EPL queries are created and stored in the engine. Statement examples for the benchmark tests are listed in the following:

Tests for filtering (query depth = 1):
  select * from EventA where EventA.attributeA = 'RED';
Test for transformation (query depth = 2):
  select attributeC as averageSize, attributeC as profession
  from EventC.std:lastevent() as attributeC, EventD.std:lastevent() as attributeD
  where EventC.eventId=EventD.eventId
Tests for event pattern detection (query depth = 3):
  select * from pattern [every data= EventA (attributeA='green')
  -> (EventB (attributeB = EventB.attributeB))
  -> (EventD (attributeD1>3000))]";

3.2   Benchmark Results

Because the workload varies in different CEP applications, there is no typical workload proposed. In this demonstration, we set the work model as the following: The workload is composed of 500 event batches, which each batch has 20,000 events. The average of interval times is set to 0.3 seconds.

Table 1. Parameter values for different test groups

Settings	Group1	Group2	Group3
number of query statements	10	100	100
the depth of query statements	1, 2, 5	1, 2, 5	3, 5

Considering the factors we discussed in the Section 2.4, we set up three groups of tests according to the factors which we consider influence the system performance. The query depth of a type of query statements is fixed: Filtering statements have depth as 1; Transformation statements have depth as 2; Event pattern statements have two depth settings which are 3 and 5. The performance tests are categorized into three groups (the Table 1): The Group 1 is testing the three functional behaviours respectively with 10 query statements; The Group 2 is testing the functional behaviours respectively with 100 query statements; And the Group 3 is testing the effect of window size factor on the system performance. The Group 1 and the Group 2 are designed for revealing the performance effect of different functional behaviours. No windows are implemented in the statements in these two test groups. The Group 3 is designed for revealing the effect of depths of querying event history. Time windows and length windows are applied for performance comparison study.

The input throughput, output throughput and response time are measured. The input throughput and output throughput are measured as events per second. The averages of input throughput and output throughput are calculated and presented. The response time is measured in milliseconds. Relative frequencies and cumulative distribution of response time are calculated and presented.

Response Time of Test Group 1. The Figure 4 depicts the relative frequency and the cumulative distribution of response time for filtering, transformation and pattern detection in the test Group 1. The relative frequency distribution is divided into two parts in order to show the curve clearly. The part of the distribution that goes beyond the visible part of the graph is not displayed here. The response times of filtering are mainly in the interval between 0 and 15 milliseconds (the Figure 4a). The response times of transformation are mainly in the interval between 0 and 40 milliseconds (the Figure 4b). The relative frequency distribution for event pattern detection has both a higher mean and higher variability (from 0 to 350 seconds) than the other query types (the Figure 4c). This is because the system takes considerable time to query on event history and wait for the pattern to be matched.

The Figure 4d presents a cumulative distribution comparison for filtering, transformation and pattern detection in the test Group 1. The part of the distribution that goes beyond the visible part of the graph is not displayed. The cumulative probabilities of response time for filtering and transformation con-

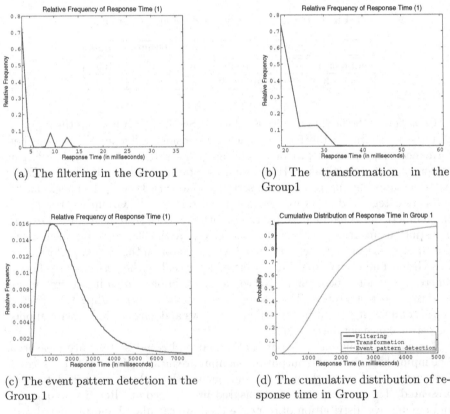

(a) The filtering in the Group 1

(b) The transformation in the Group1

(c) The event pattern detection in the Group 1

(d) The cumulative distribution of response time in Group 1

Fig. 4. The relative frequency and the cumulative distribution of response time in Group 1

verge to 1 sharply and overlap with each other, while the response time for pattern detection converges to 1 slowly.

The results in Group 1 reveal that the Esper engine responds faster in filtering than in transformation, and it responds faster in transformation than in event pattern detection.

Response Time of Test Group 2. The Figure 5 illustrates the relative frequency and the cumulative distribution of response time for filtering, transformation and event pattern detection in the test Group 2. The relative frequency distribution is divided into two parts in order to show the curve clearly. The part of the distribution that goes beyond the visible part of the graph is not displayed here. The relative frequency distribution for filtering are mostly in the interval between 0 and 50 milliseconds (the Figure 5a). The relative frequency distribution for transformation has a higher variability than filtering with a peak probability of about 0.08 between 160 and 200 milliseconds (the Figure 5b). The relative frequency distribution for event pattern detection has both a higher

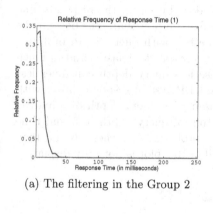

(a) The filtering in the Group 2

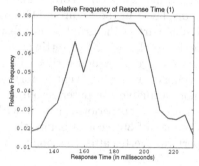

(b) The transformation in the Group 2

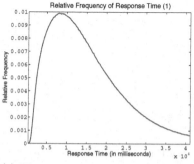

(c) The event pattern detection in the Group 2

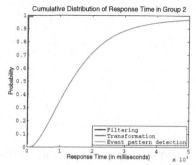

(d) The cumulative distribution of response time in test Group 2

Fig. 5. The relative frequency and the cumulative distribution of response time in the Group 2

mean and higher variability (from 0 to 2000 seconds) than the other query types (the Figure 5c).

The Figure 5d depicts the cumulative distribution of the response time for filtering, transformation and event pattern detection in the test Group 2. The part of the distribution that goes beyond the visible part of the graph is not displayed. Similarities are found with the cumulative distribution of response time in the test Group 1. The cumulative probabilities of response time for filtering and transformation converge to 1 sharply, while for event pattern detection it reaches 1 slowly. The long tail of this plot is not fully displayed.

The results in Group 2 prove the conclusion of the test Group 1 that the Esper engine responds faster in filtering than in transformation, and it responds faster in transformation than in event pattern detection.

Results of Test Group 3. To explore the performance impact of query depth and window sizes, we set up the test Group 3, in addition to the test Group 1 and 2. The benchmark application is run with a hundred of event pattern statements respectively: with the query depth of 3, no windows and the query depth of 5, time windows of 30 seconds. The cumulative distribution of the response time is displayed in the Figure 6. The part of the distribution that goes beyond the visible part of the graph is not displayed. The test with query depth of 3 outperforms the other two settings, as the curve converge to 1 faster and in much lower range of response time. This is because less query depth consumes less memory for keeping event history so that the CEP system responds faster with more available computer resources. The system with query depth of 5 and no windows is outperformed by it with the setting of query depth of 5 and time windows of 30 seconds before the cumulative probability reaches 0.6 and then performs better after this point. The long tail of this plot is not fully displayed.

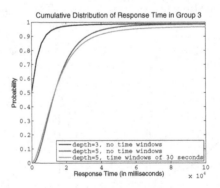

Fig. 6. The cumulative distribution of response time in the test Group 3

Comparison of Response Time with the Factor of Query Load. The Figure 7 shows the cumulative distribution of response time for filtering, transformation and patter detection under different query load in Group 1 and Group

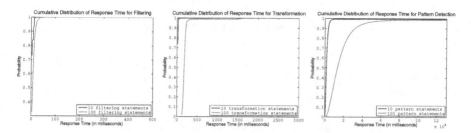

Fig. 7. Comparison of response time for filtering, transformation and patter detection with different query load

2 tests. Three graphs are included in this figure. They demonstrate that query load influences the system performance. Tests with heavier query load have larger response time.

System Input Throughput in the Tests. The Figure 8 shows the system input throughput in the test Group 1. The input throughput is sampled and measured in each event batch. The system is run for 3 times and the average of the input throughput is calculated and plotted. The input throughput of filtering fluctuates considerably between 140,000 events/second and 210,000 events/second. However, it is much higher than the input throughput of event pattern detection and transformation overall. Noticeably, the input throughput of event pattern detection is higher than the input throughput of transformation.

The Figure 9 presents the input throughput of test Group 2. The input throughput is sampled and measured in each event batch. The system is run for 3 times and the average of the input throughput is calculated and plotted. The input throughput of filtering fluctuates between 52,000 and 58,000 events/second, which is much higher than the input throughput of the transformation and event pattern detection in the same group. However, it is significantly lower than the input throughput of filtering in the Group 1.

The Figure 10 shows the system input throughput in the test Group 3. The input throughput curves of the query depth 3 without time windows and the

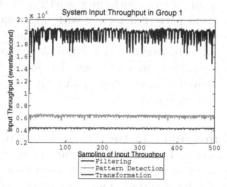

Fig. 8. The system input throughput in the test Group 1

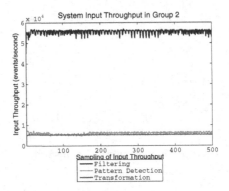

Fig. 9. The system input throughput in the test Group 2

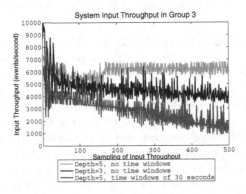

Fig. 10. The system input throughput in the test Group 3

query depth 5 with time windows of 30 seconds are declining because of increasing memory consumption and garbage collection, while the curve for the query depth 5 without time windows becomes steady after a period of decline. Overall the input throughput with the query depth 5 and no time windows outperforms the other two. However, this is not expected. The tests with query depth of 5 and no time windows is supposed to perform worse than the tests with the other two settings, because event pattern detection with higher query depths usually consumes more memory. This phenomenon needs more investigation.

The major reason for the fluctuation of the input throughput curves is relating to the garbage collection activity and CPU activity during the simulation. The input events will be removed from the system after they are processed, and this triggers garbage collection in the system.

System Output Throughput in the Tests. Outputting events consumes resources of CEP systems. Output load and output throughput can indicate how heavy the processing work is engaged in CEP engine with the input workload and the scalability of the CEP system. Our test environment does not strictly control the amount of output, because values of event properties and values in

Table 2. The system output throughput and output load in the test Group 1 and Group 2

Functionalities	Output of Group 1		Output of Group 2	
	Throughput (events/sec)	Load (events)	Throughput (events/sec)	Load (events)
Filtering	14431	3,077,108	84366	28,821,616
Transformation	15031	6,248,000	28644	58,731,250
Event Pattern Detection	3119	990,876	5508	11,086,190

Table 3. The system output throughput in the test Group 3

Settings (100 event pattern statements)	Output Throughput (events/sec)	Load (events)
Depth=3, no windows	6932	19,598,140
Depth=5, no windows	5508	11,086,190
Depth=5, time windows of 30s	2606	10,891,536

query statements are generated with a random process. Table 2 and 3 present the average output throughput and the average output load in three test groups.

Comparing the output load and output throughput of three functionalities in Table 2 of the Group 1 and Group 2, it is found that the scalability of filtering in Esper engine is the best among the three functionalities. The output throughput and the output load of filtering are both nearly eight times more in Group 2 than in Group 1. The output load of transformation and event pattern detection in Group 2 are nearly ten times heavier than they are in Group 1, while the output throughput of transformation and event pattern detection are nearly twice larger in Group 2 than they are in Group 1.

3.3 Summary

The results of performance tests by running the CEPBen on Esper CEP engine are presented in this section. The functional behaviours of Esper CEP engine are evaluated. The cumulative probability distribution of response time for filtering, transformation and event pattern detection presented in the Figure 4d, 5d and 7reveals the similarities and differences in response time with the three functional behaviours. Factors which influence system performance are tested. System input and output throughput are measured, presented and compared. The performance study demonstrates that the CEPBen is able to classify the performance of the functional behaviours and explore the effects of factors.

4   Related Work

A fundamental aspect for performance evaluation is performance metrics. The scenarios of applied event processing range broadly and have different operational requirements in terms of throughput, response time, type of events, patterns, number of event sources and consumers, scalability, and more. Common performance metrics of interest are the expected event notification latency, utilization and message throughput of the various system components [14].

Throughput is a critical metric to show the ability of systems to handle large amount of data. Mendes et al. take throughput as the metric and conducted a series of tests to compare the performance of three event processing systems [17]. Lakshmanan et al. [15] choose throughput to demonstrate that their novel approach could achieve high scalability especially when the model and network topology change frequently. Throughput measurement is also applied in the paper by Wu et al. [20]. A complex event system, SASE, is developed to address the need of sliding windows and value-based comparisons between events in monitoring applications using radio frequency identification (RFID) technology. Their work focus on high volume streams and extracting events from large windows. Oracle published a white paper on the performance of Oracle Complex Event Processing. The output event rate which is output throughput, average latency, 99.99% latency and absolute max latency are the metrics in the performance tests [2]. In addition, Isoyama et al. evaluate the throughput as the performance metric for their scalable context delivery platform in their paper [13].

Latency is the time that a system takes for the output events to emerge after the input event happened. It is one of the important metrics in the performance evaluation in traditional information systems, while it is not often found in the literature of complex event processing. Grabs and Lu [12] presented information latency and system latency as metrics for event processing systems to address the challenges of out-of-order arrival events. The system latency is well understood as it is the time that a system takes to process the events. The information latency is caused by delays that the CEP system spends waiting for additional input.

Some novel metrics are found in the literature. In Linear Road benchmark [4], response time and supported query load are proposed as appropriate metrics for the system. Sustainable throughput, response time, scalability, adaptivity, computation sharing, and similarity search and precision and recall are considered to be useful metrics in the BiCEP benchmark [5]. However, many of these metrics are yet to be implemented and demonstrated in event processing systems.

Several benchmarks are proposed in different fields related to event processing. However, benchmarks of CEP systems are rarely found in the literature. In this section, we review three benchmarks in the related fields.

SPECjms2007 [18] (Standard Performance Evaluation Corporation) is a benchmark to provide a standard workload and metrics for measuring and evaluating the performance and scalability of Message-Oriented Middleware (MOM) platforms based on Java Message Service (JMS). It provides a standard workload and performance metrics for competitive product comparisons, as well as a framework for in-depth performance analysis of enterprise messaging platforms.

The linear road benchmark has been created for Stream Data Management Systems (SDMS) by Arasu et al. [4]. It simulates a toll system for motorways, where tolls are set according to dynamic factors, such as traffic congestion and accident proximity. It is designed to evaluate the performance of the systems to respond the real-time queries in processing high-volume streaming and historical data.

BEAST (BEnchmark for Active database SysTems) is a benchmark for active Database Management Systems (ADBMSs) [11]. It is based on the OO7 benchmark, which was built for performance tests of Object-Oriented Database Management Systems (OODBMS) [6][7]. BEAST benchmark tests active functionality of active database systems. It can be used to compare the performance of multiple ADBMSs and identify the performance weakness of their systems compared with others.

SPECjms2007 provides standard workload to measure performance and scalability of JMS based MOM platforms. Linear Road is a popular workload of traffic and transportation. Both of them do not focus on the system functional behaviours. BEAST has a series of tests for rule execution and events detection in active database systems. However, complex event processing applies event-condition-action (ECA) rules concepts, but goes beyond ECA in term of complexity of events, conditions and actions [8]. Our benchmark CEPBen is to evaluate the performance of event processing behaviours which involve complex events, conditions and actions in complex CEP systems.

5   The Conclusion and Future Work

In this paper, we present the CEPBen benchmark for complex event processing systems on the system functional behaviours: filtering, transformation and event pattern detection. We introduce the benchmark design, implementation and its features of flexibility for exploring the factors and metrics of performance of CEP systems. Following the benchmark design, we create a benchmark application that is run on Esper CEP engine. We present the results of performance tests for the three functionalities and influential factors. We demonstrate that CEPBen is capable of classifying the performance of CEP functional behaviours and investigating influential factors in CEP systems.

In the future, we will apply the CEPBen benchmark on other CEP engines, and explore metrics and influential factors for performance of CEP systems.

References

1. Esper performance (2007), `http://docs.codehaus.org/`
2. Oracle complex event processing performance (November 2008), `http://www.oracle.com/`
3. Oracle complex event processing exalogic performance study - an oracle white paper (2011), `http://www.oracle.com/`
4. Arasu, A., Cherniack, M., Galvez, E., Maier, D., Maskey, A., Ryvkina, E., Stonebraker, M., Tibbetts, R.: Linear road: A stream data management benchmark. In: VLDB Conference (September 2004)
5. Bizarro, P.: Bicep - benchmarking complex event processing systems. In: Chandy, M., Etzion, O., von Ammon, R. (eds.) Event Processing, Dagstuhl, Germany. Dagstuhl Seminar Proceedings, number 07191, Internationales Begegnungs- und Forschungszentrum für Informatik (IBFI), Schloss Dagstuhl, Germany (2007)

6. Carey, M.J., DeWitt, D.J., Naughton, J.F.: The 007 benchmark. SIGMOD Rec. 22(2), 12–21 (1993)
7. Carey, M.J., DeWitt, D.J., Kant, C., Naughton, J.F.: A status report on the oo7 oodbms benchmarking effort. In: OOPSLA 1994: Proceedings of the Ninth Annual Conference on Object-Oriented Programming Systems, Language, and Applications, pp. 414–426. ACM, New York (1994)
8. Chandy, M.K., Etzion, O., Ammon, von Ammon, R.: 10201 executive summary and manifesto–event processing. Event Processing (10201) (2011)
9. EsperTech Inc. Esper Reference, version 4.9.0 edition (2012)
10. Etzion, O., Niblett, P.: Event Processing in Action. Manning Publication Co., Stamford (2011)
11. Geppert, A., Gatziu, S., Dittrich, K.R.: A designer's benchmark for active database management systems: 007 meets the beast. In: Sellis, T.K. (ed.) RIDS 1995. LNCS, vol. 985, pp. 309–326. Springer, Heidelberg (1995)
12. Grabs, T., Lu, M.: Measuring performance of complex event processing systems, pp. 83–96 (2012)
13. Isoyama, K., Kobayashi, Y., Sato, T., Kida, K., Yoshida, M., Tagato, H.: A scalable complex event processing system and evaluations of its performance, pp. 123–126 (2012)
14. Kounev, S., Bacon, J., Sachs, K., Buchmann, A.: A methodology for performance modeling of distributed event-based systems. In: 11th IEEE Symposium on Object Oriented Real-Time Distributed Computing (ISORC) (2008)
15. Lakshmanan, G.T., Rabinovich, Y.G., Etzion, O.: A stratified approach for supporting high throughput event processing applications. In: DEBS 2009: Proceedings of the Third ACM International Conference on Distributed Event-Based Systems, pp. 1–12. ACM, New York (2009)
16. Luckham, D.C.: Event Processing for Business: Organizing the Real Time Enterprise. John Wiley & Sons (2011)
17. Mendes, M.R.N., Bizarro, P., Marques, P.: A performance study of event processing systems. In: Nambiar, R., Poess, M. (eds.) TPCTC 2009. LNCS, vol. 5895, pp. 221–236. Springer, Heidelberg (2009)
18. Schmidt, A.R., Waas, F., Kersten, M.L., Florescu, D., Manolescu, I., Carey, M.J., Busse, R.: The xml benchmark project. Technical report, Amsterdam, The Netherlands (2001)
19. Tibbetts, R.: Performance & scalability characterization, http://www.streambase.com
20. Wu, E., Diao, Y., Rizvi, S.: High-performance complex event processing over streams, pp. 407–418 (2006)

Author Index

Printed in the United States
By Bookmasters